GUIDE TO
AMERICA–HOLY LAND
STUDIES
1620–1948

AMERICA—HOLY LAND STUDIES

Project Director and General Editor	Moshe Davis
Co-Directors	Selig Adler Robert T. Handy
Editorial Coordinators	Nathan M. Kaganoff, U.S.A. Menahem Kaufman, Israel

A Joint Project of the
American Jewish Historical Society
Ruth B. Fein, President
Lloyd H. Klatzkin, Chairman of the American
Jewish Historical Society-Institute of
Contemporary Jewry Liaison Committee
Bernard Wax, Director, American Jewish Historical Society
and the
Institute of Contemporary Jewry
The Hebrew University of Jerusalem
Daniel G. Ross, Chairman of the Institute's
International Planning Committee
Mordechai Altshuler, Head, Institute of Contemporary Jewry
Yehuda Bauer, Academic Chairman,
International Planning Committee
Lucy D. Manoff, Coordinator, U.S.A.

GUIDE TO AMERICA–HOLY LAND STUDIES
1620–1948
VOLUME 4

Resource Material in
British, Israeli and Turkish Repositories

Edited by
Menahem Kaufman and Mira Levine

Introduction by
Moshe Davis

PRAEGER SPECIAL STUDIES • PRAEGER SCIENTIFIC

New York • Philadelphia • Eastbourne, UK
Toronto • Hong Kong • Tokyo • Sydney

Library of Congress Cataloging in Publication Data

Main entry under title:

Guide to America–Holy Land Studies, 1620–1948.

    Includes index.
    Contents: –v.4. Resource Material in
British, Israeli and Turkish Repositories
      1. Palestine–Library resources.   2. United States–
Relations–Palestine–Library resources.   3. Palestine–
Relations–United States–Library resources.
I. Kaufman, Menahem II. Levine, Mira
Z3476.G84   1984   016.95694   82-13322
ISBN 0-03-071653-5 (v.4)

Responsibility for publication	Nathan M. Kaganoff
Responsibility for British material	Vivian D. Lipman
Responsibility for Turkish material	Jacob Landau

Ongoing research is supported by
The Jacob Blaustein Fund for American Studies,
Mrs. Rosemary Ehrenreich Krensky, Dr. Miriam Freund Rosenthal, and
Dr. and Mrs. Benjamin M. Stein

Published in 1984 by Praeger Publishers
CBS Educational and Professional Publishing,
a Division of CBS Inc.
521 Fifth Avenue, New York, NY 10175 USA

©1984 by Praeger Publishers

456789 052 987654321

Printed in the United States of America
on acid-free paper

In tribute to
Harry Starr
for his lifetime of service and
devotion to learning

PREFACE

The uniqueness of Volume 4 of the *Guide to America-Holy Land Studies, 1620-1948* lies first and foremost in its considerable expansion and deepening of our access to the multifaceted documentation housed in the archives of Israel. Second, British repositories previously unexamined for America-Holy Land material are impressively recorded. Finally, we are afforded a tantalizing glimpse of the heretofore untouched Ottoman resources in Turkish repositories.

In the Israeli collections, the abundance of documentation from the period of the British Mandate, 1920-1948, attests to more than is indicated by the mere proximity in time. The explanation is manifold: American interest and involvement in the Mideast greatly increased following World War I, as the United States emerged from its self-imposed isolation to assume world leadership. An early manifestation of this interest concerned oil concessions in the area. Concomitantly, the political, economic and even demographic status of the Jewish community in both America and Israel changed radically in the 30 years preceding the establishment of the State of Israel. As the *yishuv* grew and stabilized, American Jewry's interest in Eretz Israel intensified while the membership and activities of the Zionist movement in America expanded. Political and financial support for the *yishuv* gradually became the norm among American Jews, Zionist and non-Zionist alike. Intensification of the Arab-Jewish conflict and the struggle of the *yishuv* against the Mandatory authorities forced both American Jews and the United States government to take stands. All the above factors coalesced to generate an abundance of America-Holy Land documentation from the early 1920s onward. These provide the bulk and fiber of the entries in this volume.

Compilation of the entries has underscored the indispensability of Israeli archival material to America-Holy Land research. The collections at the Central Zionist Archives, Yad Ben Zvi Archives and Israel State Archives in Jerusalem as well as the Jabotinsky Institute and Hakibbutz Hameuhad Archives in the Tel Aviv area contain documents crucial to our understanding of this complex subject. Our researchers in Jerusalem have listed the major holdings of the Yad Ben Zvi Archives, as well as over 60 private collections in the Central Zionist Archives, thereby completing the examination of this repository. For the first time we have addressed ourselves to the thousands of promising files at the Israel State Archives, both those of the Mandate government and private holdings paralleling or preceding them. Many record groups have been examined, but several major collections remain untapped.

No less valuable is the pertinent material culled by our researchers from repositories in the Tel Aviv area. Virtually all 400 collections of the Jabotinsky Institute in Israel were searched. The official correspondence, reports and memoirs of kibbutz and labor leaders were also systematically examined at Hakibbutz Hameuhad Archives in Ramat Efal. The obviously divergent views represented in the holdings of these major repositories cannot be ignored by any serious researcher of America-Holy Land relations during the first decades of the twentieth century.

This supplementary volume, however, by no means exhausts all relevant material in Israeli archives. Valuable collections yet to be examined at the Israel State Archives include the private files of Arab and Jewish lawyers, the Palestine Papers of the British Foreign Office and Colonial Office (on microfilm) as well as pre-Mandate Turkish material. The Weizmann Papers in Rehovot must be examined for all years excepting 1914-1920, which are registered herein. Nor have we even touched the literally millions of items recently made available at the Ben Gurion Archives at Sde Boker in the Negev.

Our work in preparing Volume 4 followed the model adopted in previous volumes of the *Guide*. The pattern of work was ably designed by Dr. Nathan M. Kaganoff. In his capacity as editor of the series, he has also guided our formulation and editing of the text itself and served as liaison with the publisher. We are sincerely grateful for his unstinting aid.

The procedure involved examination of pertinent institutions, collection-by-collection, and registration of record groups containing pertinent material. Each description is followed by the initials of the researcher who examined the files and prepared the entry together with the month and year when the data was gathered. The use of document and file registration forms for this volume greatly facilitated the recording of data and formulation of descriptions. An alphabetical subject index follows the text, as in previous volumes. The cumulative index to Volumes 1-4, included in this publication, promises to increase access to documents on America-Holy Land relations for specific topics of interest.

We gratefully acknowledge the contribution of Professor Moshe Davis, overall director of the project, whose skilled guidance helped us overcome the inevitable difficulties of cross-oceanic team work. Thanks are certainly due Mrs. Ora Zimmer, Mrs. Rivka Demsky, Mr. Yohai Goell and Mr. Bernard Wax, Director of the American Jewish Historical Society, all of whom meticulously reviewed various drafts of the manuscript. Their comments and suggestions have been most valuable. We are also grateful for the services of Sharon Langa, Janet Lieber and Melna Charin, whose typing of the various drafts of the work greatly facilitated its preparation.

Jerusalem, Israel   Menaham Kaufman
March, 1984   Mira Levine

LIST OF RESEARCHERS

The names of the researchers, responsible for the accompanying descriptions, and whose initials follow each item, are:

Rosalind Arzt
Samuel Ashbel
Stuart Cornberg
Adina Feldstern
David Frost
Sylvan Ginsburgh
Tsafrit Greenberg
Sophie Haber
Hinda Hoffman
Mindy Ivri
Simone Kessler
Hannah Koevary
Mira Levine
Vivian D. Lipman
Mim Kemal Öke
Deborah Price
Danby Ring
Frieda Sochen

LIST OF REPOSITORIES

ANGLO-JEWISH ARCHIVES, University College London, Gower Street, London WC1, England

ARCHEOLOGICAL (ROCKEFELLER) MUSEUM, Ministry of Education and Culture, Department of Antiquities, P.O. Box 586, Jerusalem, Israel

BOARD OF DEPUTIES OF BRITISH JEWS, Woburn House, Upper Woburn Place, London WC1H OEP, England

BODLEIAN LIBRARY, Oxford, England

BRITISH AND FOREIGN BIBLE SOCIETY, Bible House, 146 Queen Victoria Street, London EC4, England

CENTRAL ZIONIST ARCHIVES, King George Avenue, Jerusalem (mailing address: P.O. Box 92, Jerusalem 91000, Israel)

HAKIBBUTZ HAMEUHAD ARCHIVES, Ramat Efal, Ramat Gan, Israel

ISRAEL FILM ARCHIVES, Jerusalem Cinematheque, Wolfson Garden, Hevron Road, Jerusalem (mailing address: P.O. Box 4455, Jerusalem 91043, Israel)

ISRAEL LABOR PARTY ARCHIVES, Bet Berl, Tsofit - Kefar Saba 44905, Israel

ISRAEL STATE ARCHIVES, Government Office Buildings, Hakirya, Jerusalem, Israel

JABOTINSKY INSTITUTE IN ISRAEL, 38 King George Street, Tel Aviv, Israel

JEWISH NATIONAL AND UNIVERSITY LIBRARY, Givat Ram Campus, P.O. Box 503, Jerusalem, Israel

LAMBETH PALACE LIBRARY, London SE1 7JU, England

OTTOMAN STATE ARCHIVES, Sirkeci Quarter, Istanbul, Turkey

PALESTINE EXPLORATION FUND, 2 Hinde Mews, Marylebone Lane, London W1, England

PUBLIC RECORD OFFICE, Ruskin Avenue, Kew Gardens and Chancery Lane, London WC2, England

RHODES HOUSE LIBRARY, Oxford, England

ST. ANTHONY'S COLLEGE MIDDLE EAST CENTRE, Oxford
OX2 6JF, England

TEL AVIV-YAFFO MUNICIPALITY HISTORICAL ARCHIVES,
27 Bialik Street, Tel Aviv, Israel

THEATER ARCHIVES, Mexico Building, Tel Aviv University, Tel
Aviv, Israel

UNIVERSITY OF BIRMINGHAM LIBRARY (Helsop Room),
c/o Sub-Librarian, Special Collections, University Library,
P.O. Box 363, Birmingham BI5 2TT, England

WEIZMANN ARCHIVES, Weizmann Institute, Rehovot, Israel

YAD YITZHAK BEN ZVI, 17 Ibn Gabirol Street, Jerusalem 92430,
Israel

INTRODUCTION

Foremost in the publications program of the America-Holy Land Studies Project is the archival *Guide*. The first three volumes, edited by Nathan M. Kaganoff, are: *American Presence* (New York: Arno Press, 1980); *Political Relations and American Zionism* (New York: Praeger, 1982); *Economic Relations and Philanthropy* (New York: Praeger, 1983). This fourth source book focuses on record groups in British and Turkish repositories, and on sections in Israeli archives not recorded in the previous volumes.

Details of organization and methods adopted by the research teams in the United States and Israel in our survey of some 60 repositories are described by Dr. Kaganoff in his prefaces to the previous volumes. The annotative technique developed for the *Guide* has opened many vistas of research and teaching, particularly to younger scholars. While the selected themes suggest methodological compartmentalization, the references in the several volumes reveal substantive interconnections. They illuminate vital archival information that is often tucked away in unsuspected folders or appended notes, and significant evaluative material widely dispersed in many collections. Annotation also features what may be called "correlative documentation," i.e., where unpublished sources disclose previously unknown or neglected aspects of the historical endeavor and cast new light on the roles of individuals and institutions. The cumulative record of the *Guide* is replete with such evidence, which will inevitably compel reexamination of major themes in the America-Holy Land relationship.

Connections between the English and American record come amply to the fore in this volume as, for example, references to American missionary reports found in the British material (the British and Foreign Bible Society, Church Missionary Society, Malta Bible Society). Pliny Fisk's letters from Jerusalem (April 1824) and from "Beyrout" (June 27, 1825) also abound in descriptions of local conditions in the respective cities, and contain details of his acute problems with Turkish police and magistrates. A jointly signed letter (September 1, 1824) from William Goodell and the American,

xiv   *Guide to America-Holy Land Studies*

Isaac Bird, to the British and Foreign Bible Society includes the English translation of the Sultan's firman and ban of the BFBS's Bibles.

Of even greater significance is new information indicating the need for re-evaluation of accepted historical positions. Many of these sources deal with the early stages of the current Arab-Israel conflict. The George Antonius Papers referred to in this volume are one striking source. Another noteworthy document on this subject is the full report in Hebrew by Yitzhak Ben Zvi, later second president of the State of Israel, recounting his diplomatic closet meeting with Colonel Harold B. Hoskins (January 13, 1943). Hoskins had been sent on a fact-finding mission to the Middle East covering Iraq, Iran, Transjordan, and the Arab communities of Palestine. In their intimate conversation, Ben Zvi emphasized the Zionists' abiding concern for the mitigation of the areas of conflict between the Arab and Jewish peoples, and stressed that the immediate removal of Great Britain's White Paper of 1939 would be a boon for cooperative solutions.

Documents and marginal notes relating to Lord Balfour, wherein his cross-current views on the Zionist position are fully reflected, reveal politically pertinent statements that may involve reconsideration of the historical record. Such evidence runs between his eloquent greeting to the American Zionist Medical Unit in 1918 and the comment on an interoffice communication "need we publish this balderdash?" At the same time, the files reveal—again through marginal handwritten interpolations on the face of official reports— the important role played by Louis D. Brandeis in shaping Balfour's public position on the British role in Palestine.

The sequence seems to be as follows: On April 24, 1917, Brandeis wrote to Jacob De Haas: "I met Balfour at the reception last evening. As soon as he heard my name, his face brightened up and he said: 'I have heard much of you and I want to have a talk with you.' I told him to summon me when he had the time and I shall probably hear from him soon. . . ." The very morning he dispatched that letter, Brandeis met with Sir Eric Drummond, who had accompanied Lord Balfour to Washington. At that session, Drummond ascertained from Brandeis that the objective of the Zionists was "to obtain equal rights and opportunities for Jews in Palestine, combined with the maintenance of the autonomy which the present local Jewish institutions there enjoy" (typed on Foreign Office stationery June [no date] 1917). The following marginal note in Drummond's handwriting (and signed E.D. 18.6.17) brings the major change in Balfour's thinking to light. "I should be inclined *not* to send this. Mr. Brandeis had a later interview with Mr. Balfour, when I believe he took up a much more definite attitude than he did in my conversation with him. He advocated a national home for the Jews in Palestine under a British protectorate and I understand received promises of Mr. Balfour's personal support for the Zionist Movement."

Additional archival nuggets recorded in this collection are the Yiddish letters of Ben Gurion written in the United States to his party associates, and his exchanges with leading members of the World Zionist Executive (e.g., the correspondence with Rabbi Solomon Goldman of Chicago in the critical months of March-April 1939). They illuminate his unique leadership qualities: indefatigable attention to detail; penetrating observations on organizational weaknesses; sacrificial commitment to his assumed responsibilities; effervescent intellectual curiosity.

The scope of the materials culled from British, Israeli and Turkish repositories and annotated in this volume reflects the international nature of the America-Holy Land Studies Project. While it was apparent from the outset that the many archives in the U.S. and Israel would have to be thoroughly surveyed, the number of repositories in Great Britain and Turkey requiring extensive research is far greater than we had expected. In due course, we may also branch out to such European countries as Germany, France and Austria, primarily because they maintained consular relations with the Holy Land. Thus, the continuing quest for relevant material in European and Middle Eastern repositories has proved indispensable to the historical study of America-Holy Land relations.

Jerusalem, Israel   Moshe Davis
March, 1984

AARONSOHN FAMILY

(Among founding families of Zikhron Yaakov; Aaron, Alexander and Sarah founded NILI intelligence organization during World War I; Aaron, an agronomist, established the Jewish Agricultural Experimental Station at Athlit in 1910.)

2 items, covering years 1927, 1929, in Record Group 1.

In Tel Aviv-Yaffo Municipality Historical Archives, Tel Aviv.

Items consist of copies of letters from Alexander Aaronsohn to Julius Rosenwald in Chicago concerning the Jewish Agricultural Experimental Station at Athlit (File 6; originals in the Aaronsohn Archives at Zikhron Yaakov).

Collection catalogued by repository.

Research access not restricted. Photocopies provided.

SA 5/82

AFRICAN EXILES' ARCHIVE

(The 254 detainees from Jewish resistance groups arrested in Palestine by the British authorities and exiled to Kenya without charge or trial in 1947.)

3 items, dated 1948, in Record Group K 15.

In Jabotinsky Institute in Israel, Tel Aviv.

Items consist of copies of three letters to Meir Grossman and others, including the American delegation to the United Nations, from Arie Mehoulal, seeking American intervention on behalf of repatriation to Palestine of the detainees in Kenyan exile (Folders 4/10,20,27).

Collection catalogued by repository.

Research access not restricted. Photocopies provided.

SA 2/82

AKZIN, BENJAMIN, 1904-
(Born in Latvia; professor of constitutional law and political science at Hebrew University; head of political division of New Zionist Organization and director of its Washington office 1936-1941; secretary of American Zionist Emergency Council 1945-1947.)
Ca. 100 items, covering years 1939-1945, interspersed in Record Group PA 15.
In Jabotinsky Institute in Israel, Tel Aviv.

Collection includes correspondence, reports, press interviews and newsclippings regarding activities of Akzin and the New Zionist Organization in the United States; efforts toward formation of a Jewish army during World War II; rescue of European refugees; the American Zionist Emergency Council; political events in Palestine; and meetings with United States Senators (e.g., Claude Pepper, Henry Cabot Lodge, Jr.) and American officials.

Also included is correspondence with the World Zionist Organization and the National Council of Jewish Women as well as an interesting exchange in which Akzin unsuccessfully attempts to persuade Felix Frankfurter to meet with Zev Jabotinsky.
Collection catalogued by repository.
Research access not restricted. Photocopies provided.

TG 12/81

AMERICAN BIBLE SOCIETY (ABS)
Numerous items, covering years 1855-1890, interspersed in American Bible Society Papers.
In British and Foreign Bible Society, Bible House, London.

Collection includes the papers of ABS agent at Constantinople, Isaac Bliss (1857-1889), and correspondence with American missionaries in Syria, George C. Hurter and Henry Harris Jessup.
Collection catalogued and indexed.
Research access not restricted. Prior arrangement advised. Photocopies provided.

VL 1/82

AMERICAN COLONY IN JERUSALEM
(Established in 1881 by a group of American Christians from Chicago led by Horatio and Anna Spafford; later augmented by Americans of mainly Swedish extraction; organized handicrafts and health

and educational institutions; incorporated in 1928; located to this day in the Sheikh Jarrah quarter of East Jerusalem.)
1.   Ca. 160 items, covering years 1914-1923, in chronological folders in Record Group 12.
In Yad Yitzhak Ben Zvi, Jerusalem.

Collection contains detailed correspondence in English and records in Arabic concerning the interest of Americans in the small sect of approximately 200 Samaritans in Nablus; letters between E. K. Warren, a philanthropist from Three Oaks, Michigan, and John D. Whiting, U.S. Vice Consul in Jerusalem and member of the American Colony.

Included are requests for economic aid for the American Colony; descriptions of conditions in Jerusalem and Eretz Israel during World War I; reactions in the United States to situation in Eretz Israel; and information on methods of sending money from the United States to Eretz Israel during the war (Folder 12/2/1/1).

The history of the Samaritan Committee in the United States under the chairmanship of E. K. Warren and his philanthropic efforts on behalf of the Samaritans is documented in Folders 12/2/1/2-10.

Among the correspondents are Ambassador Henry Morgenthau, Sr.; Mr. Larsen and Mr. Jones of the American Colony; Professor Goodrich of Albion College; Max Killner of the Episcopal Theological School of Cambridge, Mass.; Jacob Schiff of the Jewish Relief Fund; Walter Smith of the United States Department of State; James Morgan, editor of the *Boston Globe*; Charles E. Correy of Yale University; Professor Alan Montgomery of the University of Pennsylvania; and the Provisional Executive Committee for General Zionist Affairs in New York.

Of special interest are the following letters in Folder 12/2/1/9:

from John D. Whiting (September 6, 1915) describing the work of the Samaritans and life at the American Colony;
from E. K. Warren (June 12, 1915) describing the work of the Samaritan Committee;
from Warren (February 8, 1916) discussing purchase of land in Nablus;
from Whiting (December 17, 1918) to the Military Governor in Jerusalem summarizing the relationship between Warren and the Samaritans; and

from Whiting (May 12, 1922) to the District Governor of Samaria summarizing his relationship with the Samaritans.

Collection not catalogued; arranged chronologically by researcher. Research access not restricted. Photocopies provided.

HH 5/82

2.   Ca. 200 items, covering years 1870-1930, in photographs in a separate album and interspersed in the following collections: Miss E. Blyth, Humphrey Bowman, Monckton, Bishop Popham Blyth, Jerusalem and East Mission.
In St. Anthony's College Middle East Centre, Oxford.
    Collections of photographs include albums, sets of photographs and lantern slides by American Colony photographers, notably G. E. Matson and F. Vester:

18 prints by Bonfils and American Colony of Jerusalem (Vester), ca. 1870-1890 (E. Blyth);
15 sepia photographs of Jerusalem street scenes, Al Aksa mosque, probably by Matson (Bowman);
45 lantern slides of Palestine 1917-1920: personalities, social and religious occasions (Monckton);
10 albumen prints of Jerusalem by Vester (Bishop Blyth);
album containing 50 early American Colony albumen prints; and
lantern slides by G. E. Matson; pastoral scenes for Bible illustrations; "Bishop Stewart's Palestine Slides"; "Customs and Peoples of the Holy Land"–44 colored slides from the years 1870-1930; similar collection in black and white from 1930; slides of such historical figures as General Edmund Allenby and Thomas E. Laurence (Jerusalem and East Mission).

Handlist in repository.
Research access not restricted. Photocopies provided in many cases.

VL 6/82

AMERICAN FRIENDS OF A JEWISH PALESTINE (AFJP)
(Zionist committee affiliated with Revisionist movement; active in various cities in the United States 1939-1943; Hillel Kook (Peter

Bergson) among its leaders; dedicated to the aim of establishing an autonomous Jewish state spanning both sides of the Jordan River.)
Ca. 185 items, covering the years 1939-1943, comprising Record Group HT 10.
In Jabotinsky Institute in Israel, Tel Aviv.
   Collection consists of correspondence and other documents relating to the following aspects of AFJP activities:

   aims, tasks and publicity of AFJP (Folders 1; 3-5; 18);
   first annual convention of AFJP at the New York Biltmore Hotel in 1940 (Folder 2);
   opposition of other American Zionist organizations and individuals to the activities of AFJP (Folders 11; 16);
   correspondence of AFJP with the British Embassy in Washington regarding activities to rescue European Jews and gain their admittance to Palestine (Folders 13; 14; 17);
   support of the Irgun Zevai Leumi (IZL) (Folders 3; 10; 11; 16);
   the New Zionist Organization of America, including the resignation of Hillel Kook (Peter Bergson) from its presidency in 1941 (Folder 12);
   local chapters of AFJP in various American cities: Philadelphia, New York, Chicago (Folders 6; 7; 8; 15); and
   organizational and fund-raising matters of the Palestine Defense Fund (Folder 15).

Collection catalogued by repository.
Research access not restricted. Photocopies provided.

SA 3/82

ANGLO-AMERICAN COMMITTEE FOR A JEWISH ARMY (CFJA), LONDON

(London office of the committee established by the Revisionists to muster governmental and Jewish support for the formation of an army of stateless and Palestinian Jews to fight with the Allied Forces in World War II.)
Ca. 600 items, covering years 1942-1945, interspersed in Record Group HT 3A.
In Jabotinsky Institute in Israel, Tel Aviv.

Collection includes telegrams, letters, memoranda, newsclippings, speeches and reports documenting the cooperation of the New York and London offices of CFJA in their efforts to bring pressure on the British and American governments and public toward achieving their aims of forming a Jewish army, rescuing the remnants of the Jewish people from Europe and establishing a refuge in Eretz Israel. The documents cover the following subjects:

> coordination between the London and New York offices in the activities of the Emergency Committee to Save the Jewish People and establishment of an emergency refugee shelter in Eretz Israel (Folders 3/29; 33; 34);
>
> dissension between the Revisionists and other American Zionist groups described by Jeremiah Halpern, Pierre Van Paassen, Edwin Johnson, Hillel Kook (Peter Bergson) and Samuel Merlin, among others (Folders 3/33; 65);
>
> encouragement by United States Ambassador John C. Winant of correspondence between the London office of CFJA and the American Embassy and a request that Second Secretary Jacob D. Bean be informed of all activities (Folder 3/50); and
>
> reactions to activities of the CFJA by ex-President Herbert Hoover, Secretary of the Interior Harold L. Ickes and president of the American Federation of Labor, William Green (Folders 3/29; 34).

Of special interest is a speech delivered September 14, 1943 at a large public meeting in London by Congressman Will Rogers, Jr., favoring the establishment of a Jewish army in which refugees, stateless and Palestinian Jews would contribute to the war effort (Folder 3/33).

Collection catalogued by repository.

Research access not restricted. Photocopies provided.

SC 10/81

ANGLO-AMERICAN COMMITTEE FOR A JEWISH ARMY (CFJA), NEW YORK
(Established by the Revisionists to organize and strengthen American governmental and Jewish support for the formation of an army of stateless and Palestinian Jews to fight with the Allied Forces in World War II.)

Ca. 5 linear feet, covering years 1939-1946, in 59 folders comprising Record Group HT 3.

In Jabotinsky Institute in Israel, Tel Aviv.

Collection consists of statements, petitions, circulars, official and personal correspondence, telegrams, financial records and other documents relating to activities of the New York office of CFJA. The leading personalities included Hillel Kook (Peter Bergson), Samuel Merlin, Eri Jabotinsky and Senator Edwin Johnson, chairman. The following subjects are discussed in the material:

1. Aims and tasks of CFJA (Folder 1/1); financial reports (Folder 1/4); activities of the many offices of CFJA throughout the United States (Folders 5/50-59); correspondence and records of outstanding workers and supporters (Folders 4/30-49).

2. Opposition by Chaim Weizmann to CFJA; the need for greater cooperation among various groups of American Zionists within and outside of the Zionist Organization of America (Folders 2/6; 3/28-29).

3. Problems posed by the eligibility of active CFJA members (Arieh Ben Eliezer, Yitzhak Ben Ami, Alexander Hadani, Eri Jabotinsky, Samuel Merlin and Peter Bergson) for the United States military draft, including correspondence with Lewis Hershey, director of the Selective Service system and Adolf A. Berle, Assistant Secretary of State (Folder 3/24).

4. Formation of the Free Palestine Committee and the American League for a Free Palestine (Folder 3/21).

5. Petitions and publicity of CFJA to private individuals and institutions as well as to the British and American governments and other embassies (Folders 1/2; 2/5,6,9-15; 3/18-20,25-27).

Of special interest are the following:

5a. 3-page printed "Proclamation on the Moral Rights of the Stateless and Palestinian Jews," dated 1942, demanding the right of these Jews to form an army to fight for the Allied Forces, followed by a 5-page list of some 2,000 supporters, including outstanding American military, political and Jewish leaders (Folder 1/2).

5b. 6-page undated [1942-1943?] survey assessing the possibility of training a Jewish army on the United States mainland (Folder 1/2).

5c. 29 issues of *Memo*, the weekly publication of CFJA, February 13, 1943-February 5, 1945 (Folder 2/9).

5d. 3-paragraph petition, dated October 1943, sent to the President and Congress of the United States and signed by ca. 640 persons (among 22 similar petitions in Folder 2/11).

The collection also contains ca. 800 refusals and acceptances to join and/or support the activities of CFJA by U.S. congressmen and dignitaries as well as foreign leaders (Folders 1/3; 3/18-27, 29,34).

Of special interest are the following:

refusals to support the committee by Herbert Hoover and Thomas Mann; acceptances to support by Secretary of War Henry Stimson and Secretary of the Navy Frank Knox (Folder 1/3);

2-page statement issued by Senator Edwin Johnson on February 24, 1943, accepting chairmanship of CFJA and explaining his reasons for doing so (Folder 1/2);

2-sentence letter from Harry S Truman to Pierre Van Paassen, dated May 22, 1942, stating that he will meet Alexander Hadani but that he is "not very strong for a Jewish Army" (Folder 3/25);

telegram from Senator Claude Pepper to Dr. Samuel Church, dated February 12, 1941, stating his support of CFJA (Folder 3/25);

2-page letter from Secretary of State Cordell Hull to Pierre Van Paassen, dated November 12, 1942, acknowledging that CFJA represented a good cause but regretting his inability to sign even an unofficial proclamation (Folder 3/26); and

telegram in French from Charles de Gaulle, dated March 2, 1943, stating the impossibility of creating a unit of stateless Jews within the Free French combat forces (Folder 3/20).

Collection catalogued by repository.
Research access not restricted. Photocopies provided.

SC 9/81

ANTONIUS, GEORGE, 1891-1942
(Author of Lebanese origin who studied the Arab nationalist movement; research fellow during 1930s of the Institute of Current World Affairs, established in New York by Charles Crane; wrote *The Arab*

Awakening (1938); cultivated close acquaintances among political and cultural elite of England and Middle East, including the Grand Mufti of Jerusalem.)
600 items, covering years 1917-1937, 1946, in Record Group 65/4, among the private papers of George Antonius in the collection of abandoned documents (1948).
In Israel State Archives, Jerusalem.

Collection contains letters, memoranda, telegrams, reports, articles, newsclippings, course outlines, itineraries and bank statements falling into two categories: private correspondence and copies of historical documents for personal use and/or for *The Arab Awakening*.

   1. Private correspondence deals with the following matters:

Antonius as research fellow of the Institute of Current World Affairs, New York: his meetings with Charles Crane, founder and financial supporter of the Institute; reports on the situation and activities throughout the Arab world (Folders 135; 704); internal Institute business, Antonius' travel itineraries, representation on committees, lectures, writing, progress reports; emphasis by Walter Rogers, New York staff member of the Institute, that Antonius must remain neutral in Palestinian affairs to be regarded an impartial observer; advice from Rogers, Charles Crane and his son John (also actively involved in the Institute) on how to relate to the American people on Arab issues (Folders 137; 704); possibility of beginning a Moslem university in Jerusalem to compete with the Hebrew University as discussed with Victor Clark of the Library of Congress and Institute staff member (Folder 2550); possibility of funding a 2-3 month stay in Palestine for James Parkes and interest in his thesis on anti-Semitism (Folder 135).

Conversations of Antonius with the Grand Mufti of Jerusalem (Folder 704); meeting of Antonius with the International Committee on Intellectual Cooperation, headed by Judah Magnes and Norman Bentwich (Folder 704); meeting of Magnes with [Charles] Crane at the home of Antonius (Folder 704); efforts of Magnes toward bringing Arabs and Jews together (Folder 137).

Visit by Antonius to the United States in 1935: arrangements, speaking engagements at various universities (Princeton, Harvard, University of Chicago, Stanford) and institutes, including a lecture at the Chicago Council of Foreign Relations several days after Zev Jabotinsky had spoken (Folders AT/12,464; 135; 130; 137).

Requests by American university professors for information on Near Eastern issues (Folder 130); requests for membership and other information from various American learned societies (Folder 131). Of note is correspondence with the American Academy of Political and Social Sciences in Philadelphia regarding the publication of their *Annals* issue devoted to Palestine and the invitation from Harry Viteles to act as co-editor that was rejected by Antonius, who recommended Dr. Khalil Totah, principal of the Ramallah Friends Boys School (Folders 137; 369).

Miscellaneous aspects of visits by Americans, publication of research and financial transactions of Antonius (Folders AT/12,464; AT/57,2740; 135; 175; 178; 866; 869). Those figuring in the correspondence include Charles Merz of the *New York Times*, Roger Straus and Arthur Hays Sulzberger with their wives, Walter Rogers regarding Walter Lippmann ("he is a Jew but I do not believe he is a Zionist—at least not a professional one"), Vincent Sheean and Wallace Murray of the State Department.

Of special interest in the above private correspondence are the following:

1a. Folders 854 and 860—correspondence between George Antonius and Charles Crane and the latter's son John during the years 1930-1936: letters (many handwritten) and telegrams dealing with Antonius' work for the Institute of Current World Affairs, the research of his book and meetings between the Cranes, either in Palestine, the United States or elsewhere. Outstanding here are letters from Charles Crane showing his constant efforts in advancing Arab causes, his personal relationship and intervention with a number of influential Arabs, in particular the Grand Mufti. Subjects, for example, include their meeting on March 16, 1933 to discuss the Executive of the Moslem Congress, plans for a Moslem university in Jerusalem, ideas for an English newspaper under Arab control in Jerusalem, relationships between Moslem and Catholic authorities in Jerusalem, including Crane's intention of raising matters of Moslem-Catholic cooperation with "high personalities in the Catholic World in Rome" (Folder 854); meeting in Cairo on November 25, 1933 with influential and intellectual Arabs at which Crane spoke of the danger to Islam by Jews coming to Palestine (Folder 860).

Charles Crane's letters to Antonius reveal strong anti-Jewish feelings, for example, his denunciation of Jewish immigration to Palestine and general Jewish presence there; his efforts to convince the Grand Mufti of problems posed by the Jews regarding Zionism and his solutions (Folder 860/April 26 and August 24, 1933).

1b. Correspondence regarding a meeting of Antonius with President Franklin Delano Roosevelt on May 1, 1935, including a 5-page report (September 20, 1935) sent by Antonius to Wallace Murray, chief of the Near East Division, Department of State in Washington; Elliot Palmer, Consul General in Jerusalem, Walter Rogers and John Crane (Folders AT/12,464; 135; 854).

1c. Letters (December, 1929-April, 1930) to Antonius from American journalist Vincent Sheean discussing the latter's confrontation with Meyer Weisgal regarding Sheean's commissioned articles on Palestine, the reversal of Sheean's previous pro-Zionist position, his appearance before the Shaw Commission, letters to Antonius describing Jewish anti-Zionist and non-Zionist activity in the United States and the positive reception of Sheean by anti-Zionist and non-Zionist Jews (Folder 1961).

1d. Letter (January 21, 1930) from Sheean suggesting that Antonius make contact with Charles Crane via Charles Merz for possible work at the Institute (Folder 1961).

2. In addition to the above private correspondence, the collection includes typewritten copies of historical documents, newsclippings and other background material apparently gathered by Antonius in researching *The Arab Awakening*. This nonoriginal material is found in Folders 2579; 2669; 2750; AT/24,858; AT/57,2740; AT/58,2758; AT/70,2753; AT/78,2727; AT/122,2710; AT/205,3260 and deals with the following subjects:

Balfour Declaration—formulation of its text, approval of text by President Woodrow Wilson and timing of official approval as reflected in cables and letters exchanged by Louis D. Brandeis, Chaim Weizmann, President Wilson and William Phillips of U.S. State Department (Folder AT/57,2740; see below, of special interest).

King-Crane Commission 1919-1922—background and development, origins in International Commission on Mandates, initiative of Howard Bliss, reports to President Wilson and his reactions, official publication of the report, background sketches on George Montgomery, William Yale, Albert Lybyer and Howard Bliss, secret arrangements between British and French on mandates; possibility/ desirability of Palestine being under U.S. mandate.

Besides Henry King and Charles Crane, correspondents and/or persons figuring in the files include President Woodrow Wilson, Donald Brodie, Howard Bliss, Albert Lybyer, Louis Mallet, M. Jean Gout, William Yale, George Montgomery (Folders AT/78,2727; AT/24,858; 2669; see below Of special interest).

Paris Peace Conference—position of U.S. Zionists; Felix Frank-furter interceding with President Wilson to approve and sponsor Balfour Declaration and establishment of the Jewish national home; meetings between Lord Balfour, Brandeis, Lord Eustace Percy and Frankfurter about Zionist program and current problems of Great Britain with France and the Arabs; boundaries of Palestine and historic Jewish claims to Palestine as stated by Zionist Organiza-tion of America and supported by American Jewish Congress (Fold-ers 2750; AT/58,2758; AT/70,2753). The collection also includes many extracts from David Hunter Miller, *My Diary at the Conference* (limited edition, New York, 1924-1926, 21 volumes, on microfilm in Israel at Jewish National and University Library, File 1358 deals with Versailles Conference) (Folders AT/58,2758; AT/78,2727).

Anglo-American Committee of Inquiry—copies of 5 book-lets on the public hearings in Jerusalem in 1946 (Folders 2604-2608, among the Antonius papers, albeit relating to events after his death).

Of special interest in this background material are copies of the following documents:

2a. Four telegrams exchanged by Louis D. Brandeis and Chaim Weizmann during September-October, 1917 discussing whether Brandeis and President Wilson would support the text of the Balfour Declaration approved by the British Prime Minister and Foreign Office; presenting amended text and stressing need for enthusiasm by Wilson and American Zionists and non-Zionists (AT/57,2740).

2b. Cable (October 16, 1917) to Eric Drummond (secretary to Lord Balfour) from Woodrow Wilson, stating that he would make his approval of the Balfour Declaration only after a public request for it by American Jews and its publication by Britain (Folder AT/57, 2740).

2c. Letter (November 30, 1934) to Donald Brodie from Charles Crane, explaining the origins of the King-Crane Commission, the initiative of Howard Bliss and the agreement by Wilson influenced by Bliss (Folders AT/24,858; AT/78,2727).

2d. Letter (July 6, 1922) to Crane from President Wilson, giving authority for public release of the King-Crane report (Folder AT/78, 2727).

2e. 5 pages of diary entries (February 28-May 29, 1919) headed "Extracts Relating to Syria–From the Diary of Albert Howe Lybyer in 1919" on organizing the King-Crane Commission (Folder AT/78, 2727).

2f. "Strictly confidential" memorandum of an interview at the Balfour apartment in Paris on June 24, 1919 with Louis D. Brandeis, Lord Eustace Percy and Felix Frankfurter; conditions for realization of the Zionist program discussed along with current problems of Britain with France, Faisal and the Arabs in general (Folder AT/58,2758).

2g. Strictly confidential statement of the Zionist Organization regarding Palestine (February 3, 1919): outline of boundaries; historic Jewish claims to the land; countries supporting Jewish claims; American Jewish Congress support in resolution of December 16, 1918; proposals to the Mandatory authority for representative government for peoples of Palestine; signed by U.S. members Julian Mack, Stephen S. Wise, Harry Friedenwald, Jacob De Haas, Mary Fels, Louis Robison, Bernard Flexner (Folder AT/58,2758).

2h. Two reports (1917-1919) regarding the possibility of U.S. protectorate over Syria, including points to be presented to the Peace Conference and League of Nations; opposition to dividing Syria into three segments with Palestine in the south to be administered by Zionists under the British (Folder AT/122,2710).

Collection also contains newsclippings or typed copies of articles on American support for Zionist endeavors in Palestine that appeared during 1917-1919 in the *London Times* (Folders AT/57, 2740; AT/58,2758; AT/78,2727); and in 1922 in the *New York Evening Post* (Folder AT/78,2727).

Collection catalogued by repository.

Research not restricted. Photocopies provided.

HK 11/82

ARLOSOROFF MURDER TRIAL, NON-PARTISAN COMMITTEE FOR THE DEFENCE

(New York committee for the defence of Abraham Stavski, Zevi Rosenblatt and Abba Ahimeir, accused of assassinating Chaim Arlosoroff in June, 1933.)

Ca. 3/4 inches of material, dated 1934, in a special folder in Record Group HT 8.

In Jabotinsky Institute in Israel, Tel Aviv.

Folder 39 of the collection contains correspondence, memos, minutes of meetings and appeals of the committee, whose members included Jacob De Haas (chairman), Chaim Tchernowitz, Ida Landau; matters of fundraising for the defence and contributions by Americans are discussed.

Collection catalogued by repository.

Research access not restricted. Photocopies provided.

TG 11/81

AUSTER, DANIEL, 1893-1963

(Mayor of Jerusalem; born in Galicia; practiced law in Jerusalem from 1920; appointed deputy acting mayor 1935-1938, 1944-1945; served as mayor 1948-1951.)

Ca. 27 items, covering years 1947-1948, interspersed in Record Group A297.

In Central Zionist Archives, Jerusalem.

Collection includes correspondence, memos and reports regarding the status of Jerusalem; the American delegates to the United Nations committee to draw up a statute for Jerusalem in December, 1947-January, 1948 (Folders 35 and 41); and Auster's speaking engagements in the United States by invitation of Stephen S. Wise regarding the United Nations debate on partition (Folder 35).

Collection catalogued by repository.

Research access not restricted. Photocopies provided.

SG 10/81

BEN AVI, ITHAMAR, 1882-1943

(Journalist and Zionist; son of Eliezer Ben Yehuda; editor of *Doar Hayom*, *The Palestine Weekly* and publisher of *Deror*; spent World War I in United States engaged in Zionist activities; attaché to the Zionist delegation at the Versailles Peace Conference.)

Ca. 400 items, covering years 1917-1943, interspersed in Record Group 5/2.
In Yad Yitzhak Ben Zvi, Jerusalem.

Collection contains correspondence, some in Hebrew, and a printed brochure and announcement regarding American visitors and settlers in Eretz Israel; Felix Warburg in 1924, 1932 (Folders 6/8; 23/41); Louis Bienstock, Reform rabbi from New Orleans, in 1933 (Folder 3/14); Mortimer Lieberman, "the engineer who was prominent in the draining of the Emek" and Mrs. Archibald Silverman, owner of an orange grove, in 1932 (Folder 6/8); Dr. Ginsburg, mentioned in a Hebrew document as traveling to Eretz Israel in 1928 to represent a group of Springfield, Massachusetts Jews who invested $40,000 in orange groves in Herzliya (Folder 5/20); Nathan Kaplan, president of the American Jewish Association of Palestine (Folder 26/47); Israel Kligler in 1929 (Folder 6/1); William F. Albright in 1928 (Folder 21/22); Charles Passman in 1924, director of the American Zion Commonwealth (AMZIC) (Folder 23/41); and others (Folders 3/17; 6/23; 17/29; 23/41; 26/18,23; 27/15; 34/49,52; 38/54).

Material relating to American colonies at Balfouriya, Herzliya and Afula include correspondence between Emile Berliner of Washington, Charles Passman and Ben Avi relating to purchase of land by Berliner in Balfouriya in 1924 through AMZIC (Folders 9/14; 16/6; 30/30; 34/38); and correspondence in Hebrew dated 1928 from Oved Ben Ami, representative of the Bnai Binyamin organization in the United States, to Ben Avi concerning purchase of land in Herzliya by Americans, particularly the group from Springfield, Massachusetts (Folder 15/20). Ben Avi was suggested as the AMZIC representative in Egypt (Folder 36/20).

Of special interest is an 11-page pamphlet (October 24, 1937) in honor of Bernard Rosenblatt departing for his fifteenth trip to Eretz Israel, containing information on Balfouriya, Afula, American funds for redemption of the Haifa Bay area, American involvement in the Tel Aviv Bond issues in 1922 and in the Tiberias Hot Springs Co. (Folder 46/2).

The collection also contains correspondence, bulletins and announcements concerning Ben Avi's speaking tours in the United States on behalf of the Jewish National Fund (JNF) 1936-1941 (Boxes 9;12;18;21;27;38;40;44); the Palestine Development League

(PDL) 1923-1924 (Boxes 4; 9; 18; 39; 40); other Zionist organiza-
tions 1923-1924, 1936-1937 and early 1940s, including the United
Palestine Appeal (UPA), United Jewish Appeal (UJA), the Zionist
Organization of America (ZOA) and Hadassah. Correspondents in-
clude Mendel Fisher, Mordecai Rudensky, Jacob De Haas, Meyer
Weisgal, Louis Lipsky, Louis Schwefel and Stephen S. Wise.

Also includes material referring to the Palestine Restoration
Fund in 1919 (Folder 17/55); Zionist activities of Louis D. Brandeis
and his disagreement with other Zionist leaders (Folders 9/7; 12/33;
36/33; 44/39; 46/3); dissension between Chaim Weizmann and
Stephen S. Wise at the Zionist Congress at Basle in 1931 (Folder
6/84); *New York Times* correspondent Joseph Levy and Louis Lipsky discussing *Hadoar* articles criticizing Arthur Ruppin in 1923 and
the subsequent dispute between Ruppin and Ben Avi (Folders 34/35;
39/23; 40/8); the request by Ben Avi in 1941 to interview the
"greatest lady of the United States" [Eleanor Roosevelt] and tell
her about Eretz Israel (Folder 4/7).

Of special interest are the following:

2-page letter (February 9, 1919) to Ben Avi from Benjamin V.
Cohen on behalf of Jacob De Haas, thanking Ben Avi for his
work for the Zionist Organization in America and London in
connection with the Versailles Peace Conference (Folder 4/52);
2-page letter correspondence between Jacob De Haas and Ben
Avi concerning Louis Marshall's call for a conference at the
Astor Hotel in New York on February 17, 1924 to discuss
enlarging the Jewish Agency to include non-Zionists and forming a consolidated investment company to promote the economic development of Eretz Israel; De Haas (February 4, 1924)
expresses his opposition to Marshall's proposals and Ben Avi
(February 8, 1924) objects to De Haas' opposition to enlarging
the Jewish Agency (Folder 36/31); and
1-page letter (April 22, 1926) to Ben Avi from Louis Lipsky,
discussing the beginnings of the United Palestine Appeal and
arrangements for Ben Avi to work for the organization (Folder
9/14).

There is also correspondence and a printed booklet and contract
relating to the following matters:

The Palestine Development League (PDL) and Palestine Cooperative Co.: mainly correspondence between Jacob De Haas and Ben Avi about speaking engagements during a tour of the United States by Ben Avi on behalf of PDL (Folders 4/20; 9/7,14; 34/53; 40/19); references to various projects of PDL, including the Rutenberg hydroelectric project (Folder 18/26); correspondents also include Stephen S. Wise, Bernard Heller (Folder 39/9); Joseph Kun (Folder 40/18) and Follette Isaacson (Folders 4/7; 40/20).

The Hebrew Commonwealth Loan Program proposed in 1924 for the American Zion Commonwealth, its promotion by Bernard Rosenblatt and support by Felix Warburg (Folder 23/41).

The right, contracted in October 1923 by Ben Avi, to sell lands on a commission basis for the American Palestine Real Estate Agency while he was in the United States (Folder 46/1).

Subscriptions by Americans in 1940-1943 to the Eliezer Ben Yehuda dictionary and donations by Americans toward its publication, including several references to a fund for this purpose established by the Central Conference of American Rabbis and the Ithamar Ben Avi Fund; correspondents include Solomon B. Freehof, Felix Levy, Mordechai Lipis, Maurice Wertheim, Hemda Ben Yehuda (Boxes 4 and 5; Folders 16/56; 17/8; 27/54).

Ben Avi's experiment with writing Hebrew in Latin characters discussed in correspondence with Americans and subscriptions to his newspaper *Deror*; correspondents include Tamar de Sola Pool, who registers the disinterest of Hadassah executive members in the project (Boxes 2; 3 and 6).

Publication in the United States in 1926 and serialization in the Yiddish and Anglo-Jewish press of novels by Ben Avi and a request by Meyer Weisgal that Ben Avi write a history of the Jewish National Fund for *New Palestine* (Folders 6/46; 9/14).

Handlist of all folders available in repository. Catalog in preparation. Research access not restricted. Photocopies provided.

AF 5/82

BEN HORIN, ELIYAHU, 1902-1966
(Active Revisionist in the 1930s; came to the United States in 1940; member of the presidency of the New Zionist Organization of America (NZOA) 1940-1945; from 1944-1950 cooperated with

former President Herbert Hoover on the Hoover Plan; adviser to the Emergency Committee for Zionist Affairs.)
Ca. 90 items, covering years 1931, 1940-1947, interspersed in Record Group P 36.
In Jabotinsky Institute in Israel, Tel Aviv.

Collection contains newsclippings and articles by Ben-Horin; his personal documents; correspondence documenting NZOA activities, financial matters and Ben Horin's resignation from the presidency; correspondence between Benjamin Akzin and Ben Horin regarding influence of American oil interests on the United States Government and work within the Republican Party on behalf of Zionism; and correspondence with Ruth Gruner and Helen Friedman regarding the trial and execution of Dov Gruner.

Correspondents also include Abba Hillel Silver, John Henry Patterson and Emanuel Neumann.
Collection catalogued by repository.
Research access not restricted. Photocopies provided.

TG 12/81

BEN ZE'EV (ABRAMOVITCH) FAMILY
(Among the early settlers of the Rishon le-Zion area.)
2 items, covering years 1914-1920 and 1947, in a special folder in Record Group 5/11.
In Yad Yitzhak Ben Zvi, Jerusalem.

One item consists of a description in Hebrew by Israel Yekutieli, emigré to the United States from Eretz Israel during World War I, of his Zionist activities in the United States during the years 1914-1920 and his contacts with American Jewish and Zionist leaders Emanuel Neumann, Horace M. Kallen, Israel Goldberg, Louis Lipsky and others (Folder 1/37). The other item is a letter (1947) in Hebrew from Nathan Meirovitch to Hagit Klorfine, discussing the possibility of producing a film in Hollywood depicting the situation in Eretz Israel (Folder 1).
Collection catalogued by repository.
Research access not restricted. Photocopies provided.

AF 4/82

BEN ZVI, YITZHAK, 1884-1963
(Second president of the State of Israel; immigrated to Palestine

from Russia in 1907; deported during World War I; went to the United States where he reestablished Hechalutz together with David Ben Gurion in 1915; volunteered for the Jewish Legion in 1918 as a means of returning to Palestine and was active in mobilization of other volunteers.)

Ca. 260 items, covering years 1912-1933, interspersed in Record Group 1, among the papers of Yitzhak Ben Zvi.

In Yad Yitzhak Ben Zvi, Jerusalem.

Collection includes correspondence, mostly in Hebrew and Yiddish, a newspaper article and notes dealing with: the Achwa society for cooperative colonization in 1924 and its 30th anniversary celebration in 1944 (Folders 3/9/1/3; 3/9/2/10; 4/3/13; 4/4/23); the beginnings, development and functions of Magen David Adom (equivalent of Red Cross) in Eretz Israel, as reported to Poalei Zion in the United States (Folders 4/4/21—photocopies from American Jewish Archives); Americans participating in Jewish Legion and settlement of ex-legionnaires at Tel Adashim (Folders 4/3/20; 4/4/24; 5/5/1; 9/1/2); the biography of Joseph Binyamini as it appeared in the *Yidisher Velt* in Cleveland, his arrival in the United States, in 1912, membership in Poalei Zion, participation in the Jewish Legion, other Zionist socialist activities in the United States (Folder 6/1/1); and the conference of American Jewish Legion in Philadelphia in 1922 (Folder 6/1/2).

Of special interest is a letter (September 21, 1919) in Hebrew signed by Nellie Straus, then American Zion Commonwealth (AMZIC) representative in Palestine, addressed to soldiers terminating service with the Jewish Legion. It states that despite severe difficulties the work of providing facilities for 100 prospective ex-soldiers had begun and AMZIC would guarantee employment to every settler at Tel Adashim (Folder 5/1/1).

Most of the relevant material in the collection revolves around activities of Poalei Zion in the United States and Eretz Israel (Folder 4/1-4):

Programs, conferences, financial situation, organizational problems and publications of Poalei Zion (Folders 4/1/3,7,32; 4/3/13; 4/4/17,26,27);

lectures at Poalei Zion branches in the United States by Ben Zvi in 1915-1916 (Folder 4/4/17) and by David Ben Gurion in 1916 (Folder 4/4/11,17);

Dispute at the 13th conference of Poalei Zion in Jaffa in 1919 as to whether the official language of the organization should be Hebrew or Yiddish, with the American representative supporting Yiddish (Folder 4/3/20);
independent offer in 1923 by Milwaukee Poalei Zion to extend a loan to Merhavia (Folder 4/3/48); requests by Poalei Zion in Eretz Israel for aid from Poalei Zion in the United States (Folders 3/3/45; 4/3/42,43,45,46,51,54,56);
Hechalutz activities in U.S. cities in 1916 (Folder 4/4/17); and Workmen's Fund (or KAPAI — Kupat Poalei Eretz Israel): its establishment, financial problems, cooperative companies, relationship with Gerwerkshaften, problem of acknowledgement as representing U.S. companies (Folders 3/3/15; 4/3/12-15,19,40,42,48,59).

Of special interest among the Poalei Zion material is a 24-page booklet in Yiddish containing the program of Poalei Zion of America as adopted at their first convention in Baltimore, December 23-26, 1905 (Folder 4/1/18).
Other subjects appearing in the collection include the following:

SHILA organization to further Jewish colonization in Eretz Israel, founded in 1908 by the Buchmil family; visit of Suzanna Buchmil to the United States in 1909 to promote the organization while her husband went to Russia for the same purpose (Folders 4/1/5; 4/4/2; 4/4/28);
mission of Henry Morgenthau, Sr., to Turkey in 1918 (Folder 4/4/17 in Yiddish); and
historical memorandum on Eretz Israel and its population submitted to the Anglo-American Committee of Inquiry in 1946 (Folder 6/1/17).

Correspondents with Ben Zvi include Nahum Alkush, David Ben Gurion, Rachel Yanait Ben Zvi, David Block, Elias Gilner, Isaac Hamlin, Berl Locker, Clement Marmor, Maurice Nissim, Joseph Sprinzak, David Wertheimer and Baruch Zuckerman.
Of special interest are 2 pages of typed notes in Hebrew by Ben Zvi (January 13, 1943) on his meeting with Colonel Harold B. Hoskins, Franklin Delano Roosevelt's envoy to the Middle East and

especially to Ibn Saud, at which they discussed whether military confrontation with the Arabs was unavoidable and if so, whether the Jews would require military assistance from the United States (Folder 6/14/9).

Collection catalogued by repository. Computer access available. Research access not restricted. Photocopies provided.

FS and TG 8/81-8/82

BERKSON, ISAAC B., 1891-1975
(American educator; director of the Jewish Agency Department of Education in Palestine 1928-1935; member of Jewish Agency Executive 1931-1935; director of the research department of the American Zionist Emergency Council until 1946.)
Ca. 3 linear feet of material, covering years 1917-1948, interspersed and in special folders in Record Group A 348.
In Central Zionist Archives, Jerusalem.

Collection includes personal and official documents, correspondence, invitations, manuscripts of articles, newsclippings, minutes of meetings and financial records concerning American educators in Eretz Israel, especially for the years Berkson resided in Jerusalem (1928-1935). Activities of his family (Folders 12; 15; 19; 25; 29; 82; 95; 103) and American Zionist leaders, visitors, including Maccabiah Games participants (Folders 9; 10) and immigrants to Eretz Israel, especially Jewish educators and teachers, are also documented.

Berkson's role as director of the Jewish Agency Department of Education in the transfer of education to the local authorities (Vaad Leumi) and as a member of the Jewish Agency Executive during the years 1928-1935 is found in Folders 9-13; 15; 26; 28; 29; 32; 34; 52; 68; 99; 100; 104. Aid by Berkson to visiting and immigrant teachers, particularly the employment of American teachers/educators in Eretz Israel, is found in Folders 9-12; 27; 29; 97.

There is also correspondence of Berkson and his wife with American Zionists and/or educators who visited/resided in Eretz Israel, including Henrietta Szold, Jessie Sampter, Albert and Bertha Schoolman, Horace M. Kallen, Judah L. Magnes, Stephen S. Wise, Abba Hillel Silver and Maurice Karpf (Folders 9-12; 15; 25; 26; 28; 29; 52; 71; 81; 83; 96; 97), and especially Alexander and Julia Dushkin (Folders 9-12; 15; 25; 100).

Of special interest are several handwritten letters from Alexander Dushkin to Berkson (1920-1921) in which Dushkin describes his activities in Jerusalem and advises Americans not to come just yet "unless with finances or some special skill"; comments what "havoc morally the existing system of American *halukah* (traditional stipend distributed among Jews in Eretz Israel) has wrought"; discusses his impressions of Jewish life and leadership in America and in Eretz Israel; comments on his early associations with Henrietta Szold, Jessie Sampter, Julia Aaronson (later Dushkin) and other Americans then in Jerusalem (Folder 15).

The collection also includes personal and official correspondence, reports, invitations, articles, speeches, radio scripts and minutes of meetings concerning the following subjects:

Americans reporting political events in Palestine 1917-1920, including the Sykes-Picot Agreement, the Paris Peace Treaty and the King-Crane Commission (Folders 20; 36; 37), and the Arab riots of 1929 (Folder 83).

ESCO Foundation and ESCO Fund activities, including Freedom Village, the Neumann Study, the Jordan Valley Authority and the ESCO Palestine Study as well as Berkson's association with Frank and Ethel Cohen (Folders 16-18; 24; 33; 59-63; 65; 69; 72-79).

Pro-Zionist activities of the Christian Council for Palestine (Folders 17; 56; 64; 74).

Organization and expansion of activities of the Jewish Agency in the early 1930s (Folders 9; 10; 20; 29).

Activities and materials of the American Zionist Emergency Council and its research department, directed by Berkson (Folders 17; 18; 23; 24; 32; 33; 36; 37; 51; 56; 57; 61; 71; 97).

Berkson's Zionist activities in the United States, including extensive lecturing and writing of articles about Eretz Israel, especially the structure and development of its educational system (Folders 9-13; 15; 26; 28; 29; 32; 33; 51-53; 66; 68; 70; 89; 91).

Internal dissension within the Zionist Organization of America (ZOA) and between the World Zionist Organization (WZO) and ZOA in 1921; Louis D. Brandeis versus Judah L. Magnes; Chaim Weizmann versus Jacob De Haas; De Hass versus Aaron Aaronsohn; and Edmond de Rothschild versus Weizmann (Folder 20).

Various projects and activities in/for Eretz Israel sponsored by Hadassah during the second quarter of this century, e.g., playgrounds in the 1920s, Junior Hadassah and Masada (Folders 9-12; 15; 20; 29; 51; 100).

Eretz Israel as an important element in American Jewish education and in the establishment of the Council for the Reconstruction of Jewish Life in America under the leadership of Mordecai Kaplan (Folders 9; 35; 47; 68; 91).

Correspondence to and from Louis D. Brandeis on various aspects of American relations with Eretz Israel, 1917-1936 (Folder 20).

Correspondents in the various files also include Julian Mack, Julius Simon, Felix Frankfurter, Chaim Weizmann, Baron Edmond de Rothschild, Louis Lipsky, and Stephen S. Wise.

Of special interest among the documents pertaining to Zionism are the following:

Memo (December 9, 1919) from Louis D. Brandeis to Julian Mack expressing lack of confidence in the ability and character of Judah Magnes but willingness to invite him to a proposed meeting with Jacob Schiff if Jacob De Haas, Julian Mack and Stephen S. Wise think it advisable (Folder 20).

7-page memo (August 24, 1920) from Brandeis to De Haas entitled "On Zeeland," setting forth Brandeis' views on the work in Eretz Israel the ZOA should support: land purchase, provision for public utilities, economic development (e.g., Balfouriya, Anglo-Palestine Company, Jewish Colonial Trust, reforestation and research as opposed to immigration and education) (Folder 20).

Memo (April 24, 1917) to De Haas from Brandeis, reporting his first contact with Lord Balfour in Washington, D.C. (Folder 20).

2-page letter (May 4, 1931) to Robert Szold from Berkson, expressing his disappointment in ZOA policy that health and education is secondary to colonization: "I am sure that Zionism in America is in the main supported directly or indirectly by the work of rabbis, Jewish educators and laymen who have had Jewish educational experience and for these groups the support of education in Palestine is a central element in the whole idea of the upbuilding of the country" (Folder 12).

2-page undated typewritten proposal for a book entitled *Palestine in the Middle East: The Road to Jewish Statehood*, jointly authored by Berkson and James G. McDonald, a history and analysis of events in the Middle East before and during the British Mandate up to the establishment of the State of Israel (Folder 9).

17-page transcript of a radio program (March 13, 1945) entitled "What is Justice for Palestine?". Participants included Berkson, Dr. Philip K. Hitti of Princeton University; interviewers were Alexander Forkner, Samuel Landau, J. Catiba; it comprised one session of the *Free Speech Forum* radio series sponsored by the Newspaper Guild of New York (Folder 33).

Finally, the collection also contains correspondence, reports and minutes of meetings on the following aspects of cultural relations:

> activities of the American Committee for the Department of Education at the Hebrew University and subsequently of the Department of Education (Folders 9-12; 15; 28; 29; 52; 68; 81); adaptation of the Binet Intelligence Test for Eretz Israel by American-trained psychologist May Bere Mereminsky (Folders 9-11);
>
> distribution in America of *Pesiot* magazine on educational problems in the elementary grades, published irregularly in Jerusalem 1926-1935 (Folders 11; 15);
>
> Americans active in establishing a model high school in Jerusalem (Folders 11; 15);
>
> Epstein Memorial Fund for books on education at the Hebrew University (Folders 10-12);
>
> Bezalel Society for Promoting Arts and Crafts in Palestine (Folder 9);
>
> United Synagogue of America and other American involvement in a committee for construction of the Yeshurun Synagogue and Center in Jerusalem (Folders 9-11; 29); and
>
> American participation in the Maccabiah Games in the early 1930s (Folders 9; 10).

Of special interest are the following:

> letter (August 14, 1944) from Berkson to Abba Hillel Silver, concerning the right of liberal rabbis to perform marriages in Eretz Israel (Folder 33);

3-page letter (April 30, 1931) from Berkson to Louis D. Brandeis, stressing the need for some Diaspora support for education: "Either the Jewish Agency or some other Diaspora agency such as Hadassah and WIZO must carry the burden. Both . . . seem inclined to accept this task but for the next year Hadassah would not be able to help us in view of the difficult financial situation in the United States" (Folder 12);
39-page report and recommendations by Berkson (February, 1929), entitled "Organization and Administration of the Department of Education of the Palestine Zionist Executive" (Folder 34);
letter (April 4, 1937) handwritten by Mordecai Kaplan to Berkson, regarding the Hebrew University's invitation to Kaplan to teach for two years (Folder 68); and
3-page letter (October 18, 1933) to Israel Kligler at the Hebrew University from Alexander Dushkin, declaring his readiness to come to help in the organization of the School of Education and of a secondary school as its school of practice (Folder 11).

Collection catalogued by repository.
Research access not restricted. Photocopies provided.

ML 11/81

BINYAMINI, YOSEF, 1879-1933
(Russian born emigré from Eretz Israel to United States in 1914; active in organizing the Agricultural Association of American ex-Legionnaires for settlement of demobilized soldiers in Eretz Israel; among first settlers in Avihail.)
Ca. 208 items, covering years 1925-1932, in Record Group 5/6.
In Yad Yitzhak Ben Zvi, Jerusalem.
    Collection includes correspondence, mainly in Hebrew, of the Agricultural Association of American ex-Legionnaires regarding routine organizational matters and problems encountered over several years in acquiring land for settlement by demobilized soldiers. Among the subjects discussed are the following:
    Efforts by members to promote the cause of the Association by arranging interviews with the High Commissioner and such *yishuv* leaders as Menahem Ussishkin, Zev Jabotinsky, Gershon Agronsky (Agron) and Berl Katznelson, among others (Folders 1/4-5B); by

sending delegates to the United States to enlist the support of ex-Legionnaires (Folder 1/5); correspondence between Binyamini in Jerusalem and members of the Agricultural Association in other parts of Eretz Israel, e.g., Eiser Tzamri-Wahl, Yehuda Leib Cohen, Dov Schohet, Meir Dubinsky (secretary of the Association in Tel Aviv), Eliezer Sherman (a delegate of the organization in the United States) and Shmuel Dov Hayyim Kris (Folders 1/5-11).

Activities of Poalei Zion and ex-Legionnaires in the United States enumerated in correspondence, some in Yiddish, with ex-Legionnaires in the United States: Benjamin Leon, Yaakov Levinson and Shlomo Friedlander (Folders 1/3,5,6,8,13).

The collection also includes a list of sympathizers of the Association including Gershon Agronsky, Yitzhak Ben Zvi and Zev Jabotinsky (Folder 1/5); draft of the constitution of the Association (Folder 1/15); correspondence regarding the rejection by Be'er Toviya of ex-Legionnaires as candidates for settlement (Folders 1/8-9); memo to PICA requesting land and financial aid for settlement (Folder 1/13); letter in Yiddish from Benjamin Leon discussing reorganization of Poale Zion in Cleveland in 1929 (Folder 1/8).

Of special interest are the following items:

Open letter in Hebrew to *Davar* (November 27, 1927) in which Binyamini accuses the executive committee of the Histadrut of neglecting the settlement of demobilized soldiers and suggests that Histadrut delegations to the United States have been reluctant to champion the cause of ex-Legionnaires for fear of damaging the general Histadrut campaign and offending various elements in the United States, such as the Workmen's Circle and labor unions (Folder 1/4).

Two editorials in Hebrew: one in *Haaretz* (June 1, 1928), criticizing the decision of the Agricultural Association to send a delegation to the United States to raise funds among American ex-Legionnaires on the grounds that separate campaigns damage the cause of Eretz Israel as a whole; the second in *Doar Hayom* (June 7, 1928) defending the delegation by presenting a short history of the Association and its problems followed by the contention that the separate campaign will not affect general fundraising because ex-Legionnaires constitute "a world unto themselves, united by their cherished traditions concerning the conquest of the homeland" (Folder 1/7).

4-page memorandum in Hebrew and English from the Agricultural Association to the 16th Zionist Congress requesting the latter to instruct the Jewish National Fund to grant them suitable lands for settlement and to include the necessary funds for settlement in their 1930 budget (Folder 1/14).

1-page memorandum (June 5, 1929) from Louis Lipsky, requesting the cooperation of the Zionist Executive in Palestine in facilitating the attendance of a representative of the Association at the Zionist Congress (Folder 1/8).
Collection catalogued by repository.
Research access not restricted. Photocopies provided.

SG and AF 3/82

BLYTH, GEORGE FRANCIS POPHAM
(Bishop of the Church of England in Jerusalem, 1887-1914.)
4 items, dated 1887 and 1914, in Record Group MS2227-2237.
In Lambeth Palace Library, London.

One item consists of a memorandum by Blyth mentioning a visit by the Bishop of Florida, whom he introduced to the Orthodox Patriarch Damianos as representing the Presiding Bishop and a hundred bishops of the American Episcopal Church (Folder MS 2232). There is also a history of Jerusalem and East Mission by its secretary from 1889-1914, Reverend William Sadler, that includes references to a Philadelphia donor of $5,000 initially and in 1902-1904 another £1,498 to the building fund of St. Mary's Girls School in Jerusalem, originally an industrial home for Jewesses. At first anonymous, the donor is later identified as Miss Welsh (Folder MS 2232/182). Also included are two letters to Bishop Blyth (September 7 and October 1, 1887) from Charles R. Hale, Cathedral Close, Davenport, Iowa about pamphlets on Eastern Church questions (Folder MS 2234).
Published catalog of collection in E.G.W. Bill, *Catalogue of MSS in Lambeth Palace* (Oxford, 1976).
Research access not restricted. Photocopies provided.

VL 6/82

BOARD OF DEPUTIES OF BRITISH JEWS
(The representative body of British Jewry; originated in 1760; concern for foreign affairs implemented jointly with the Anglo-Jewish

Association 1878-1943; had a Palestine Committee from 1929.)
Ca. 30 items, covering years 1929-1946, interspersed in Record Groups C 11 and C 14.
In Board of Deputies of British Jews, Woburn House, London.

Collection includes references to discussions between Cyrus Adler and Osmond d'Avigdor Goldsmid on Palestine (Folder C 11/2/ 24, in letter to Lucien Wolf May 28, 1929); letters, mimeographed minutes and memoranda, etc., regarding the Jewish Agency and its relations with American non-Zionists (Folder C 14/10, June 12, 1935; see below, Of special interest), Board of Deputies' relations with British Government concerning Anglo-American Committee of Inquiry in 1946 (Folder C 14/29, 30); wartime discussions on the future of Palestine, including correspondence with the American Jewish Committee (AJC) 1941-1943 (Folder C 11/2/35); a letter (January 3, 1935) to Neville Laski from Israel B. Brodie, explaining the work of the American Economic Committee for Palestine (Folder C 14/10).

Of special interest are the following:

cables (December 1 and 13, 1934) between Cyrus Adler and Neville Laski, Board of Deputies president 1933-1939, about the Jewish Agency, with references to Laski and Osmond d'Avigdor Goldsmid, Board president 1926-1933, participating in meetings of American Jewish Committee (Folder C 14/10); letter (July 17, 1935) to Felix Warburg from Neville Laski, regarding representation of Anglo-Jewry in the Jewish Agency; stating that true non-Zionists will not serve as "non-Zionist" members of the Jewish Agency; suggesting the formation of "a non-Zionist constituency in America" composed of "lovers of Palestine" paying $5 a year to elect the non-Zionist members of the Jewish Agency (Folder C 14/10); letter (July 28, 1939) to the Board, including correspondence of Leo Simon with Cyrus Adler, Stephen S. Wise and others, explaining Simon's resignation from the American non-Zionist membership of the Jewish Agency because of opposition among American Jews to partition, which Simon would have accepted (Folder C 14/14); and letter (March 26, 1943) from Richard Law, British Foreign Undersecretary, refusing the request of A. G. Brotman, secretary of the Board, to go to the United States in connection with a conference of British and U.S. governments to discuss the "refugee problem in its entirety" (Folder C 11/2/38).

Collection catalogued by repository; copy in *National Register of Archives* (NRA 19919).
Research access not restricted, but prior application required. Photocopies not provided.

VL 5/82

BRITISH AND FOREIGN BIBLE SOCIETY (BFBS), AGENTS' BOOKS

(Society founded in 1804 "to encourage a wider circulation of the Holy Scriptures"; publisher and distributor, commissioning translation and printing; employed resident agents overseas who set up Bible depots and networks of salesmen/voluntary helpers to work with the agents.)
3 items, dated 1870 and 1873, interspersed in Agents' Books Nos. 117-152.
British and Foreign Bible Society, Bible House, London.

Collection includes reports of a tour undertaken in 1870 by Alexander Thomson, agent in Constantinople, after his responsibilities were extended to include Palestine. He arrived in Jaffa "with a party of three American medical gentlemen" who joined him at Port Said and continued with him through Palestine to Smyrna and Constantinople, contributing to his pleasure, safety and the economy of his tour. In Jerusalem Bishop Gobat informed him that his supplies of Arabic scriptures came "from the Americans" (April 10, 1870).

A girls' school in Jaffa run by an American, Miss Baldwin, is mentioned in Thomson's report for the year 1873.

American Bible Society sale of Bibles affecting Bible sales from BFBS Jerusalem depot is mentioned in a letter by Thomson on August 8, 1873.
Collection indexed by writers.
Research access not restricted. Prior arrangement advised. Photocopies provided.

VL 1/82

BRITISH AND FOREIGN BIBLE SOCIETY (BFBS), FOREIGN CORRESPONDENCE
25 items, covering years 1821-1834, in Foreign Correspondence Inwards (1804-1856, 1901-1905); Foreign Correspondence Outwards (1819-1880, 1900-1906, 1919-1931).
In British and Foreign Bible Society, Bible House, London.

Collection includes BFBS correspondence with the following early American missionaries in Palestine:

Pliny Fisk—arrangements for the sale and/or distribution of BFBS Bibles in Palestine by Fisk and suggestions for various editions to be published in letters dated October 12, 1821; June 17, 1822; March 25, 1823; and December 12, 1823; William Jowett, December 12, 1823 and April 21, 1824; letters from October 24, 1823 and June 25, 1823 appear in 1824 volume because of delay in transit. Of special interest is the letter from Fisk (April 21, 1824) in Jerusalem detailing an incident when Fisk and his colleague Jonas King were arrested, for which Fisk blames the Roman Catholics.

Jonas King—account of Bibles sold in Judea and Samaria and description of a 15-day stay in Jerusalem in letters dated December 31, 1823 and May 7, 1824.

Isaac Bird—in letters dated December 10, 1827 and June 27, 1832, from Beirut.

William Goodell—in letters dated September 1, 1824; July 10, 1828 and September 1, 1825 (last also signed by American Isaac Bird), from Beirut.

Rev. Daniel Temple—in letters dated July 7, 1831; November 1, 1831; July 18, 1832; May 14, July 31, October 31, 1833 from Malta and November 19, 1834 from Smyrna.

Of special interest is a report (August 27, 1824) from BFBS agent Benjamin Barker in Beirut giving an account of the firman against the Bible and stating that "the Rev. Messrs. Bird and Fisk, American missionaries in Syria, have been the first to suffer the effects of the machinations of our enemies." Barker encloses a copy of a letter from the Rev. J. King to Peter Abbott, the Levant Company consul in Beirut, indicating the complicity of two French consuls in Syria in a scheme to have the English (and presumably the American) missionaries expelled from Syria.

The collection also includes references to help given to Americans by Damiani, the British Levant Company consular agent in

Jaffa (from Fisk in Beirut on June 27, 1825), and to the special interest of American missionaries in Armenian Christians (April 21, 1824).

Indexes for all volumes except 1901-1905.

Research access not restricted. Prior arrangement advised. Photocopies provided.

VL 1/82

BRYCE, JAMES, FIRST VISCOUNT, 1838-1922
(British statesman; writer; Ambassador to the United States 1907-1913.)
10 items, covering years 1917, 1919-1920, in Bryce Papers, USA.
In Bodleian Library, Oxford.

Collection includes two letters to Bryce from Samuel Edelman, U.S. Vice Consul in Switzerland: an undated one expressing his disapproval of the Balfour Declaration (File USA 13), the other (June 21, 1917) requesting Bryce to discuss Palestine with him (File US 23 ff 82). A letter (September 19, 1919) from Henry Cabot Lodge cites the British lack of desire for territorial acquisition in Palestine (File US 23 fol. 173).

Also included are original letters to Bryce from William Denison McCracken, U.S. journalist and editor of *Jerusalem News* 1919-1920: McCracken's request for help in getting facilities to travel with the American Mission from Boston to Jerusalem (February 24, 1919); Viscount Allenby, General Bols and others honoring McCracken for services rendered in editing *Jerusalem News* (December 16, 1919) (File USA 16); suggestion by McCracken (September 14, 1920) that Allenby, "the conqueror of Palestine without harm to Jerusalem," should be invited by American schoolchildren to the United States to counter "the attempt to use the U.S. against Britain politically" (File US 23).

Collection catalogued by repository; copy in *National Register of Archives* (NRA 6/16).

Research access not restricted, but prior admission to readership required. Photocopies provided.

VL 1/82

CHANCELLOR, SIR JOHN ROBERT, 1870-1952
(British colonial administrator; High Commissioner of Palestine, 1928-1931.)
Ca. 25 items, covering years 1928-1932, interspersed in Boxes 11-25 of the Chancellor Papers.
In Rhodes House Library, Oxford.

Collection includes correspondence regarding American reactions to the Arab riots of 1929 and subsequent events in Palestine:

Role of American Consul General Paul Knabenshue in response to the disturbances; among the correspondents are Reginald Wingate, John Shuckburgh and Lord Passfield (Sidney Webb) and Knabenshue himself (Boxes 11/7; 14/2; 16/1,4,50-51; 17/1-4; 18/2; 22/36).

American Jewry's reactions to the riots in letters from Felix Warburg, expressing disappointment with the Passfield White Paper in 1929 (Box 18/2); Isidore Arazi of New York (Box 17/1); Charles Schwager (Box 17/1 and 2), Reverend Dr. Pereira Mendes (Box 19/MF5) and Chancellor's memoirs which record his meeting with J. Goldstein, sent by American Zionists to inquire into the lack of Jewish self-defense, the appointment of the Shaw Commission and the role of Hajj Amin al-Husseini, Grand Mufti of Jerusalem, in the riots and their aftermath (Boxes 22/MF 36; 16/4; 17/1-2).

Brief visit to Palestine in 1930 by U.S. Under Secretary of Commerce Julius Klein, who reported to President Herbert Hoover his evaluation of the negative effect which the number and type of Russian and Polish Jews immigrating to Palestine had on the sympathy of Americans with the Zionist Movement (Box 18/2).

Readiness of American Jews, apprehensive about the financial future of the United States, to invest $20,000 to $30,000 in Palestine, mentioned by Chaim Weizmann in an interview with Chancellor ca. 1930 (Box 18/2).

Proposals for a solution to Arab-Jewish friction acceptable to both sides, 1929-1932, reflected in correspondence between Chancellor, Judah L. Magnes and Anglican Bishop George F. Graham-Brown. Included are memos and pamphlets regarding Brit Shalom, the Magnes-Philby proposals and Herbert Loew's proposal for a League of Lovers of Zion (Boxes 17/4; 18/2; 20/MF 12).

Chapter of Chancellor's typescript memoirs (Box 12A) on Charles R. Crane, whom Chancellor met frequently at the home of a relative; Crane's chief antipathies are cited as Bolsheviks and

Zionists, while his protégés included Arabs (Boxes 16/2; 20/MF 16).

The collection also includes the following items regarding the establishment of an English-language newspaper, the Rockefeller Museum and the financing of excavations at Megiddo:

> interview (August 17, 1932) with Gershon Agronsky, representative of Zionist Organization of America (ZOA) about a proposal to establish in Palestine a newspaper along British lines with subsequent notes on the proposal by the British Foreign News Editor and Colonial Office (Box 14/6);
> speech delivered by Chancellor at the laying of the cornerstone of the Rockefeller Museum on June 19, 1930 (Box 15/4); and
> letters from James H. Breasted and John D. Rockefeller about their planned visit to Palestine and from Field Marshal Viscount Allenby about Rockefeller financing the excavation of Megiddo by Dr. V. G. Heizer (Folder 16/2).

Collection catalogued by repository.
Research access not restricted. Photocopies provided.
(Copyright held by R. D. Chancellor, Stoke Park, Stoke Bruerne, Gowcestwer, Northants.)

VL 6/82

CHURCH MISSIONARY SOCIETY (CMS)
(Founded in 1799, active in Palestine from Malta base from ca. 1820; permanent mission in Jerusalem and Nazareth from 1851; Palestine Mission separated administratively from Mediterranean Mission in 1850.)
Ca. 100 items, covering years 1820-1934, interspersed in Record Groups C/M/0 and G3/P/0.
In University of Birmingham Library, Birmingham.

Collection contains letters and letterbooks concerning American missionary activity in the Holy Land:

> minutes of Conference of CMS local Palestine Committee, meeting monthly in Jerusalem, comprising all western missionaries and deciding the location of missionary activity in 1851, 1856-59 (File C/M/0/1-16); 1868-1890 (File C/M/0/2);

issue (1833) of *The Star in the East and Friend of Youth*, edited and published by American missionary Josiah Brewer, listing all American missionaries in Mediterranean and Middle East (File C/M/0/6/1-29);
letters from Rev. J. J. Robinson of the American Missionary Society (File C/M/0/8/23-30);
letters referring to the Jaffa visit of H. P. Childs in 1852 and missionary W. S. Schauffler of the American Board of Commissioners for Foreign Missions in 1860-63 (File C/M/0/8/57c); an invitation to Octavius F. Walton to a Jerusalem Conference (File C/M/0/8/97); W. W. Eddy, American missionary in Beirut, 1879 (File C/M/0/8/124a and 125); and
petition (1877) signed by Henry H. Jessup, W. W. Eddy, Samuel Jessup, F. A. Wood and Gerald F. Dale, Jr., against sending F. A. Klein from Jerusalem by CMS as superintendant of Mrs. Mott's British Syrian Schools, as these were in the area of American Presbyterian Board of Foreign Missions (File C/M/0/9/14).

Material on American missionaries is also found in the collection among:

incoming mail from Palestine Mission (1880-1934): contents also entered in precis books (File G3/P/P1-8); private notes on character of missionaries in area (File G3/P/P1); relationships of CMS missionaries with Bishop Blyth in 1883-1902 (File G3/P/P3); general inquiry in 1908 into missionary activities in the Holy Land area (File G3/P/P4-8); and
outgoing letters to Palestine dated 1892 (series beginning with File G3/P/L7), including a list of all western missionaries and their posts in Palestine in 1892 (File G3/P/L10).

Of special interest is a letter (1875) from Mary B. Baldwin, American Protestant Episcopal Missionary in Jaffa, concerning the possibility of appointing her nephew, Mr. Hay, to Jaffa (File C/M/0/8/96b). Collection catalogued by repository.
Research access by prior application. Photocopies provided from microfilm by Center for Research Libraries, Chicago, but not by Birmingham.

VL 1/82

CHURCH'S MINISTRY AMONG THE JEWS
(Current name of London Society for Promoting Christianity among the Jews; formed in 1809 by separation from Church Missionary Society; often called London Jews' Society (LJS).)
Ca. 20 items, covering years 1820-1919, interspersed in Record Group Dep. CMJ.
In Bodleian Library, Oxford.

Collection includes protocols (General and Sub-Committee Books) and correspondence (Letter-Books), but mostly uncatalogued bundles of miscellaneous documents relating to American missionary activities in Palestine. Included is a copy of a report of the American Board of Commissioners for Foreign Missions (ABCFM) sent by its treasurer J. Evan to LJS and agreement to exchange reports (File CMJ d. 12).

Of special interest are the following:

report (May 27, 1823) by Lieutenant H. W. Bailey of the Royal Navy from Gibraltar regarding Bibles and Testaments delivered to American missionary Isaac Bird; decision by LJS General Committee to purchase map of Palestine and present it "to American missionaries then at Malta and on their way to the Holy Land" (File CMJ d. 10/35);

letter (October, 1850) from the wife of British Consul Finn in Jerusalem to Mrs. Veitch in London, about John Meshullam (at Artas with Millerites led by Clorinda Minor): "He has just received mail from friends in America . . . and is much encouraged by the interest that persons there are taking in his efforts" (File CMJ C. 110); and

meeting in Jerusalem (February 27, 1919) attended by Bishop MacInnes, Miss Warburton, Reverend C. H. Gill and Reverend H. Sykes to discuss joint Anglo-American scheme for reorganization of missionary education in Palestine. "In the case of education for boys in Palestine, we believe the present missionary schools of CMS, LJS, Jerusalem and East Mission, and the American Alliance [all in Jerusalem] and of the American Churches at Ramleh largely meet the needs of the country. They would 'feed' the proposed Joint Missionary College" (File CMJ d. 58/9 Misc. pp. 403).

Part of the collection catalogued by repository; copy in *National Register of Archives*.

Research access not restricted, but prior admission required. Photocopies provided.

VL 1/82

DICKSON, JOHN

(British Consul in Jerusalem 1892-1906.)

4 items, covering years 1892, 1900, 1902 and 1905, in the Dickson Papers.

In St. Anthony's College Middle East Centre, Oxford, England.

Collection includes a letter concerning U.S. national, Captain Johnson, residing in Jerusalem and signatory of complaint against Dickson in which U.S. Consul Selah Merill expresses support of charges of misconduct brought by Miss Hussey (see British FO 78/54/70) against Mosche Goldstein, alias Captain Johnson (Box 2, File 6); a letter (July 4, 1902) from Sir Charles Wilson of the Palestine Exploration Fund (PEF) regarding Professor Libbey of Princeton University who conducted research in Jerusalem and presented the PEF committee in England with information concerning the best means of examining some of the Dead Sea and Jordan Valley phenomena; subsequent PEF committee proposal to establish self-recording instruments at Jaffa, Jerusalem, Jericho and in the Dead Sea to show every movement of its surface (Box 1, File 4).

Two other items are a letter (October 23, 1905) from Howard S. Bliss referring to talks with Dickson at Ramallah and Jerusalem (Box 1, File 4); a letter (April 18, 1892) from F. J. Bliss at Tel-el Hesy about refunding to Dickson money paid in connection with excavation (Box 2, File 4).

Collection catalogued by repository.

Research access not restricted. Photocopies provided.

VL 7/82

EMERGENCY COMMITTEE (JEWISH AGENCY AND VAAD LEUMI)

(Set up jointly by the Jewish Agency and the Vaad Leumi to prepare the "machinery" for the establishment of a Jewish State in Palestine 1947-1948.)

Ca. 3½ linear feet in 29 folders, covering years 1947-1948, in Record Group 41.

In Israel State Archives, Jerusalem.

Collection includes letters, telegrams, memoranda, reports and transcripts of meetings in English and Hebrew regarding:

Activities of the Jewish Agency in New York and of the Vaad Leumi in Palestine in the struggle for the passage of the Partition Plan at the United Nations and opposition to the plan by Revisionists in America. Correspondents include Moshe Shertok (Sharett) at the Jewish Agency, Eliahu Epstein (Elath), Abba Hillel Silver, Ralph Bunche and Hillel Kook (Peter Bergson) (Folder 317).

Establishment and functioning of a Provisional Council of Government for the Jewish State in the correspondence between Bunche and Shertok (Folder 317).

Organization, deliberations and reports of the United Nations Special Committee on Palestine (UNSCOP) and its activities in New York and Palestine, including testimonies of Shertok and Silver; letters to Bunche from members of the committee during their visit to Palestine with detailed personal impressions of the situation (Folders 312; 313; 317).

Activities of the Vaad Leumi in Palestine concerning *aliyah* and absorption of immigrants; selection and dispatching of emissaries to the United States; lists of supplies to be ordered from the United States to have in Palestine by May 15, 1948 (Folders 27; 263; 317).

Attitude and policies of oil companies in Palestine (Folder 317).

Attitudes of members of the United States delegation to the Security Council on immigrants to Palestine from Cyprus (Folder 317); on various proposals for Jerusalem (Folder 314); on a confidential draft (April 13, 1948) of a Trusteeship Agreement for Palestine with the United States as administering authority (Folders 313; 314); and on security problems in Palestine (Folder 312).

Other people appearing prominently in documents of the collection include David Horowitz (Folders 232; 233; 317); Dr. Hayim Greenberg (Folder 232); Arthur Lourie, director of New York office of the Jewish Agency; Robert Lovett, Under Secretary of State; Joseph Proskauer, President of the American Jewish Committee; and Trygve Lie, Secretary General of the United Nations (Folder 317).

Collection catalogued by repository.

Research access not restricted. Photocopies provided.

HH 5/82

EMERGENCY COMMITTEE TO SAVE THE JEWISH PEOPLE OF
EUROPE (ECSJP)
(Committee organized by Revisionists in the United States; aimed at
bringing pressure on the American Government and people to aid
Jewish refugees in Europe during World War II.)
Ca. 700 items, covering years 1942-1945, in Record Group HT
11.
In Jabotinsky Institute in Israel, Tel Aviv.

Collection includes correspondence, reports, publicity and
other material pertaining to American involvement in the rescue of
Jewish refugees in Europe and their settlement in Eretz Israel relating to the following:

> contacts between the International Committee of the Red Cross
> and the ECSJP regarding the evacuation of refugees from
> Europe, especially from Hungary, to Eretz Israel and the War
> Refugee Board established by President Franklin Delano Roose-
> velt (Folders 1/1-6; 2/3; 3/1,3; 5/1/3; 5/7-8; 6/1-3; 7/9; 8/4;
> 10/8);
> aims, organization and publicity of the ECSJP (Folders 1/1-7;
> 2/3; 3/2-3; 5/1/3; 5/7-8; 5/11; 6/2,3);
> American Christian condemnation of the Holocaust and sup-
> port for establishment of a Jewish state in Eretz Israel (Folder
> 8/3); and
> differences of opinion between leaders of the ECSJP and
> leaders of the Zionist Organization of America about arming
> Jewish settlers in Eretz Israel found in correspondence be-
> tween Hillel Kook (Peter Bergson) and Stephen S. Wise (Fold-
> er 7/2,4,10).

Other correspondents in the collection include Eleanor Roosevelt, Andrei Gromyko, Lipo Zabrovsky (Arie Ben Eliezer), Emanuel
Celler, and Eri Jabotinsky (Folders 3/3; 7/9; 8/3,4,9,11,14).

The collection also contains statements in 1943 by President
Franklin D. and Eleanor Roosevelt, Cordell Hull and Henry Morgenthau, Jr., that only elimination of the Nazis will ease the problem
of the Jews of Europe and enable the ECSJP to achieve its goal
(Folder 1/2).

Of special interest:

letter (September 8, 1943) from Andrei Gromyko to Max Lerner stating that he has brought the work of the ECSJP to the attention of his government (Folder 8/9); and

telegram (July 23, 1943) from Eleanor Roosevelt to Max Lerner expressing doubt that anything can be done until the war is won, though stating that whatever can, should be done for the refugees (Folder 8/13).

Collection catalogued by repository.
Research access not restricted. Photocopies provided.

SC 2/82

EPSTEIN, ZALMAN, 1860-1936
(Born in Byelorussia; settled in Eretz Israel 1925; Hebrew essayist and critic.)
1 item, dated 1924, in Record Group V 892.
In Jewish National and University Library, Jerusalem.

Item consists of a personal letter to Epstein from his childhood friend Professor Chaim Tchernowitz, Talmudic scholar from Odessa who settled in the United States and taught at the Jewish Institute of Religion in New York, expressing his yearning for Eretz Israel (File 400).
Collection catalogued by repository.
Research access not restricted. Photocopies provided.

SK 2/82

ESHED, JACOB AND FRUMA
(Emissaries of the Kibbutz movement to the United States in 1947-1948.)
Ca. 6 items, covering years 1947-1948, interspersed in Record Group 15.
In Hakibbutz Hameuhad Archives, Ramat Efal, Ramat Gan.

Collection includes memorial brochures issued by Hakibbutz Hameuhad and letters by Jacob and Fruma Eshed regarding their work in the United States; their meeting poetess Kadia Molodowsky, who expressed her desire to emigrate to Eretz Israel; and American interest in the museum of the Hehalutz Hazair at Ein Harod (Folders 1/1; 2/4; 8).

Collection catalogued by repository.

Research access not restricted. Photocopies provided.

TG 10/81

FISHER, CLARENCE S.

(Archaeologist; directed first American archaeological expedition during Mandatory period.)

1 item, covering years 1921-1923, in Record Group Ref. MS. Eng. misc. d. 129 among Clarence S. Fisher Papers.

In Bodleian Library, Oxford.

Item consists of a typescript folder of 27 pages comprising a personal account by Fisher of three seasons of excavating the ancient Egyptian settlement of Betshean (Beisan).

Collection catalogued by repository; reference in Mathews and Wainwright, *Guide to Documents in British Isles Relating to Middle East*.

Research access not restricted, but prior admission to readership required. Photocopies provided.

VL 1/82

GERMANY, CONSULATES IN PALESTINE

Ca. 43 items covering years 1868-1869, 1908, 1924-1929, and 1932, interspersed and in special folders in Record Group 67.

In Israel State Archives, Jerusalem.

Collection includes a letter and two newsclippings from the years 1928-1929 regarding transfer of the American Consulate from Beirut to Jerusalem, elevation of the mission in Jerusalem to the status of Consulate General and the appointment of Paul Knabenshue as Consul General (Folder 976 B).

Of special interest is Folder 503, which consists of ca. 40 letters, telegrams and reports from January 1868 to January 1869 regarding the intervention of U.S. Consul Victor Beauboucher when Prussian subject Arie Marcus, Rabbi of the Grand Synagogue of Jerusalem, refused to render custody of orphan Sarah Steinberg to her apostate sister Mrs. Deborah Golupsoff, an American subject. Also figuring prominently in the file is Benjamin Finkelstein, the U.S. Deputy Consul in Jerusalem.

Collection catalogued by repository.

Research access not restricted. Photocopies provided.

TG and ML 1/82

GILNER, ELIAS, 1890-1976
(American Zionist; president of Zionist Revisionist Organization of America, 1933-1935.)
Ca. 25 items, covering years 1928-1940, interspersed in Record Group P 241.
In Jabotinsky Institute in Israel, Tel Aviv.

Collection includes correspondence with Zev Jabotinsky (originals in Record Group A 1) regarding activities of the New Zionist Organization in the United States and Canada. Other correspondence discusses Jewish support of the boycott against Germany in the United States; demonstrations by American Jews against British policy in Palestine; Arab views on Palestine published in the United States by Dr. Shatara in 1934. Correspondents include various editors of American newspapers and periodicals.
Collection catalogued by repository.
Research access not restricted. Photocopies provided.

TG 12/81

GOLDMAN, SOLOMON, 1893-1953
(American rabbi and Zionist leader; president of Zionist Organization of America 1938-1940.)
Ca. 1 inch of relevant items, covering years 1939-1946, interspersed in Record Group A 296.
In Central Zionist Archives, Jerusalem.

Collection includes correspondence between Goldman and various political and cultural organizations and leaders in Eretz Israel and America concerning political developments affecting Eretz Israel; the World Zionist Organization and the Zionist Organization of America; Hanoar Haziyoni; financial assistance to institutions and individuals. Correspondents include Dov (Bernard) Joseph and Eliyahu Epstein (Elath) (Folders 2-7).

Of special interest are 4 letters of correspondence between David Ben Gurion and Goldman in March and April, 1939 discussing meetings between President Franklin Delano Roosevelt and Louis Brandeis; the positive attitude of President Roosevelt to Zionism and Eretz Israel; his efforts to influence the British Government in favor of the Jewish National Homeland via pressure from the United States Ambassador in London Joseph P. Kennedy; and the

establishment of the American Zionist Bureau in Washington, D.C., with representatives from all Zionist organizations (Folder 6).
Collection catalogued by repository.
Research access not restricted. Photocopies provided.

SH 10/81

GREAT BRITAIN, CABINET MEMORANDA AND PAPERS
(Memoranda and papers circulated in preparation for and during discussions at Cabinet meetings, 1915-1922.)
Ca. 20 items, covering years 1916-1922, interspersed in Record Group CAB 24 - Series G.T. 1-8412 (1916-1919); C.P. 1-4379 (1919-1922) and G.
In Public Record Office (PRO), Kew Gardens, London.

The collection contains communications from Colonel Edward M. House (G.T. 2015) and Louis D. Brandeis (G.T. 2158) circulated for the penultimate meeting (October 4, 1917) of the Cabinet before approval of the Balfour Declaration.

Of special interest in CAB 24/4 is Appendix III of G 164, "The Zionist Movement," circulated to the War Cabinet on October 17, 1917 and at the final meeting on October 31, 1917, when the Balfour Declaration was approved. The appendix contains a selection of extracts from documents submitted by leaders of the Zionist Organization regarding the growth of Zionism in America during World War I:

federation of American Zionists—*shekel* (dues) subscriptions and number of members in affiliated bodies: Hadassah, Zionist Union of the Western States, Young Judea Association, Poalei Zion, Order Brith Shalom—as reported at the Baltimore Conference on June 24, 1917;
financial power of Zionism in America as reflected in funds raised for relief in Palestine and other war zones; land purchase via the Jewish National Fund; and settlement, education and other work in Palestine;
American societies for cooperative purchase of land in Palestine, including the various Achooza groups, forming a union in May, 1917, with special provision for the settlement of Jewish ex-soldiers;

establishment by the Zionist movement of close relations with political elements in the United States; and

support for restoration of Palestine to the Jewish people expressed in resolutions by the Jewish Ministers Association of New York and by Jewish national, socialist, and workingmen's committees.

Subject indexes in repository for all series except G, which has numerical content lists (*PRO Handbook No. 11*).

Research access not restricted. Photocopies provided.

VL 7/82

GREAT BRITAIN, COLONIAL OFFICE (CO), PALESTINE COR-RESPONDENCE

(CO was responsible for Palestine from 1921.)

Ca. 50 items, covering years 1921-1922, 1927, 1928, interspersed in Record Group CO 733—selected themes.

In Public Record Office, Kew Gardens, London.

Collection includes correspondence between British Colonial Office (CO), Palestine High Commissioner and British Foreign Office (FO) regarding various aspects of the United States delaying its recognition of the British mandate for Palestine:

Standard Oil Company interests in Palestine—conversations in March, April and September 1920 between various officials of the U.S. London Embassy, British FO and CO and Standard Oil Company on permitting Standard Oil to continue geological explorations in Palestine covered by pre-1914 war concessions; instructions to U.S. Ambassador George Harvey to reiterate the request and state that the United States had no objection to similar explorations by other nationals. Participants included U.S. counsellor Butler Wright; Sir John Tilley of FO; L. I. Thomas of Standard Oil of New York; Sir John Shuckburgh, head of CO Middle East Department; Hubert Young of CO (File 11/September 15, 1921); Standard Oil Company claims regarding oil concessions referred to Colonial Secretary Winston Churchill for comment (File 11/September 20, 1921); concurrence of FO and CO, including Churchill, on agreement to meet United States request regarding Standard Oil; United States request for moderation of conditions denied by CO, citing inability of Palestine Government to afford geological survey, thus their desire for Standard Oil findings and control of survey for security reasons (File 11/October 16, 1921); continued pressure from United States over Standard Oil concessions: "They are plagueing my life out" (Lancelot Oliphant to Shuckburgh) and agreement to license for geological investigation with comment by Gerald L. M. Clauson of CO that while this might weaken the legal position of the Palestine Government to refuse exploitation later, they would get useful geological survey (File 30/March 25, 1922). See below, Of special interest.

Role of Lord Balfour—Fear of U.S. Zionists that mandate was to be transferred to France, reported by Balfour with reply by Shuckburgh and comment by Churchill denying any basis to rumors of either Britain considering such a move or French interest in relieving Britain of mandate (File 11/December 16 and 20, 1917); enlisting Balfour, in Washington to negotiate a naval treaty, to persuade the U.S. Government to agree to British Mandate (File 11/December 21, 1921; File 30/January 13, 1922). See below, Of special interest.

U.S. attitude to the British mandate—United States described as considering itself one of the victors over the Central Powers despite never having declared war on Turkey and thus expecting the continuance of no discrimination against U.S. nationals, missionaries or companies, and of capitulations and safeguards for U.S. nationals (File 11/December 29, 1921); concern of U.S. Government to ensure that, although not a member of the League of Nations, it should have the same privileges in Palestine as League members and the agreement of U.S. Ambassador in principle to a U.S. treaty recognizing the mandate, provided capitulations were not abrogated (File 11/April 5 and 27, May 10, 1922); report by Balfour from League of Nations meeting at Geneva, explaining that the League Council had not approved the terms of the mandate because the British Government wanted to await publication of the exchange of notes with the U.S. Government on the subject, the latter delaying their consent and claiming a voice in the mandate, that is, in the future of countries conquered in the war, despite not ratifying the Treaty of Versailles (File 34/May 17, 1922).

Elimelech Sachs case—File 146/1, dated 1928, is devoted to the Elimelech Sachs case involving 350 cases of matches received by Sachs in 1924, the day a new customs tariff increased duty on matches;

one condition for U.S. ratification of the Anglo-American Convention involved repayment of Sachs for his losses due to imposition of the duty, from which he claimed exemption under the capitulations (April 23, 1928, report by director of customs of Palestine Government; see also Great Britain, FO 371/9012, 10835, 12279).

Of special interest:

Despatch from Lancelot Oliphant in FO to CO about Standard Oil mining engineers Dana, Ley and Templeton: "While the claims of the Standard Oil Company in respect of oil concessions can only be definitely considered when the peace treaty with Turkey is ratified, Lord Curzon (Foreign Secretary) will be glad to learn the views of Mr. Churchill (Colonial Secretary) on the United States Ambassador's proposals . . . . The United States Government are deliberately making the position of His Majesty's Government in Palestine somewhat difficult by delaying the issue of the mandate for that territory and claiming to be consulted regarding its provisions" (File 11/ September 20, 1920).

Minute by Sir John Shuckburgh, blaming U.S. Government for the political status of Palestine not yet being regularized; expressing justification "in telling the Americans they must abide by the consequences of their own intransigence"; citing the small prospects of any oil being found, the opportunity to improve Anglo-American relations over Palestine and the view of Sir Auckland Geddes, British Ambassador in Washington (1920-1924), that the prospect of change in American policy ought not to be neglected (File 11/September 23, 1921).

Minute by Gerald L. Clauson of CO reporting concurrence of FO and CO officials, including Colonial Secretary Winston Churchill, on granting U.S. request regarding Standard Oil, subject to the agreement of Palestine High Commissioner Herbert Samuel, and to Standard Oil supplying the Palestine Government with a complete report of their investigation, and complying with any instructions given by the Palestine Government (File 11/October 16, 1921).

Letter (January 13, 1922) to U.S. Secretary of State Charles Hughes from Lord Balfour, attempting to hasten U.S. confirmation of the British mandate for Palestine; citing his former advocacy of the United States undertaking the mandate; strongly urging U.S. cooperation now that task falls to Britain; mentioning desire by Britain to entrust to the Jewish minority in Palestine "the task of fitting the country, with the help of outside Jewish assistance to be a home for the Jewish race," while protecting Christian ecclesiastical interests and dealing with the Arab majority; criticizing the delay in settling mandate question as weakening the position of the civilian government in the eyes of the populations concerned, thus making the difficult task almost impossible (File 30/January 13, 1922).

Collection also includes 5 items of correspondence regarding the $2 million gift for the Palestine Archaeological Museum by John D. Rockefeller; stipulations that the government donate the site and design by government architect A. St. B. Harrison; visit by Rockefeller in 1929 and the Palestine Government fixing the Megiddo road for his reception. Correspondents include High Commissioner Sir John Chancellor, CO Head of Middle East Department Sir John Shuckburgh, W. Ormsby Gore (File 146/December 9, 1927; March 8, 1929).

Collection catalogued by repository; class list CO 793.

Published catalog *PRO Handbook No. 3*.

Research access not restricted. Photocopies provided. Microfilm at Israel State Archives, Jerusalem in Record Group 123/2.

VL 8/82

GREAT BRITAIN, CONSULATE IN JERUSALEM

5 items, covering years 1893, 1895, 1910-1911, in Record Group 123/1.

In Israel State Archives, Jerusalem.

Collection includes letters and reports dealing with American citizens in Palestine:

Rolla Floyd is cited as an American subject and Mr. Kayat as a naturalized American in a letter dated 1893, and in a letter dated 1895 Floyd is reported as having his place of business in Jaffa forcibly entered (Folders 16,21).

A report headed "Statistics of passengers arriving Jaffa during season 1910-1911" cites the number of American passengers as 1,626 (Folder 12).

Collection catalogued by repository.

Research access not restricted. Photocopies provided.

TG 4/81

GREAT BRITAIN, FOREIGN OFFICE (FO), EMBASSY AND CONSULAR ARCHIVES

3 items, covering years 1823, 1824, interspersed in Record Group FO 616/1–Letter Book of Beirut Consulate.

In Public Record Office (PRO), London.

Items consist of a report (February 20, 1824) in Italian of a passport issued to Reverend Samuel Cooper, an American Catholic, to travel in Palestine; a contract in Italian (August 3, 1823), witnessed by Pliny Fisk, for lease of a house by Lewis Way and Reverend William B. Lewis for a mission to the Jews in the Levant; and a patent in Italian issued on September 22, 1824 by Peter Abbott, British Consul for Acre, Beirut and dependencies to Signor Dionisius, interpreter and dragoman of Reverend William Goodell, American missionary. The patent extends British protection for the duration of Dionisius' service in the standard form provided by the Levant company consuls under the capitulations.

Collection catalogued by repository.

Research access not restricted. Photocopies provided.

VL 7/82

GREAT BRITAIN, FOREIGN OFFICE (FO), EMBASSY ARCHIVES AND HIGH COMMISSION, EGYPT

(In 1917-1918 British Residency and High Commission in Egypt formed civil complement of British Egypt Expeditionary Force, engaged in conquest of Palestine.)

Ca. 100 pages and 10 items, covering years 1917-1918, 1919-1924, in Record Group FO 141.

In Public Record Office, Kew Gardens, London.

1. Special File 666 of the collection contains correspondence, cables and minutes of the British Embassy in Egypt dealing with the following aspects of U.S. aid to Jews in Eretz Israel during the British Palestine campaign:

1a. Advisability of inviting American aid, or accepting it if offered, and political implications of relief (Colonel Wyndham Deedes to Major Mervyn Herbert of Residency, December 4, 1917); reference to U.S. relief ship *Caesar* (telegram from London FO, January 29, 1918 in reply to Cairo telegram, December 9, 1917).

1b. Offer of $60,000 by American Jewish Joint Distribution Committee (JDC) to be distributed by U.S. Consul in Alexandria and request for report on suggested members of JDC in Jaffa and Hebron, including Eliezer S. Hoofien and Yaakov Thon.

1c. Opposition of Aaron Aaronsohn to distribution of relief by U.S. Consul, Paul Knabenshue; funds should be handed over by him to arriving Zionist Commission, "otherwise French and Italians will do it and intrigue. . . ."

1d. Criticism by Aaronsohn of Arthur Ruppin and Thon; attempts to use British authorities to exclude them from distribution of relief and to postpone action until the arrival of Chaim Weizmann and the Zionist Commission

2. Special File 435, "America and Syria and Palestine," includes ca. 10 documents of the Cairo High Commission regarding the following aspects of U.S. policy and involvement in Palestine following World War I:

2a. Request for U.S. maps, plans and guidebooks of Syria and Palestine for urgent use by the Prime Minister at the Paris Peace Conference (September 13, 1919).

2b. U.S. recognition of British mandate delayed by claim of U.S. representatives for all American rights and privileges enjoyed before World War I under capitulations in Syria and Palestine (February 27, 1921); British Government urging the U.S. Government to end demands of immunity for U.S. nationals, the only foreigners in Palestine still exercising such claims as in the case of Zaslavsky vs. Goldberg (November 29, 1923; April 16, 1924).

2c. Communications between British and U.S. governments regarding the Anglo-American Convention on Palestine and cases pending at its signature (April 30, September 2, 1924; May 9, 1925).

Collection catalogued by repository.

Published index to *Records of the Foreign Office*, *PRO Handbook No. 13*.

Research access not restricted. Photocopies provided.

VL 8/82

GREAT BRITAIN, FOREIGN OFFICE (FO), EMBASSY ARCHIVES, TURKEY

(Records of British embassy in Constantinople and British consulates in the Ottoman empire; includes correspondence with Jerusalem

consulate 1842-1914 and Haifa consulate 1899-1914; complements
Record Group FO 78.)
Ca. 150 pages and 9 items, covering years 1851-1855, interspersed
in Record Group FO 195—selected themes.
In Public Record Office, Kew Gardens, London.

Collection includes correspondence from British Consul James
Finn regarding report by the U.S. Vice Consul in Jaffa, James Kayat,
about three American families of farmers and mechanics arriving
from the United States and proceeding to Jerusalem to settle "some-
where in this country in agricultural pursuits" (File 369/March 27,
1852); augmented number of U.S. travelers in Eretz Israel (Files
369/November 7, 1851; 445/January 17, 1854); and four-week trip
to Palestine by Lord Napier of Ettrick to conduct the British Government inquiry into complaints by U.S. Consul J. Hosford Smith against
Finn's conduct (File 445/March 5 and 24, April 21, 1855).

Of special interest are the following:

Ca. 150 pages dealing with the dispute between British Consul
James Finn and the U.S. Consul for Syria and Palestine stationed at
Beirut, J. Hosford Smith, over the alleged discourtesy to U.S. Vice
Consul for Jaffa and Jerusalem, Y. S. Murad, and consular agent in
Jerusalem, S. S. Murad; the dispute between British subject John
Meshullam and the Millerite group of Clorinda Minor over property
on the Meshullam farm at Artas near Bethlehem; and intervention
by Finn in the charge of dishonesty against his dragoman, Moussa
Tannous, by U.S. missionary James Barclay in relation to purchase
of property at Wady Farah (File 369/interspersed and especially
June 30, 1852; March 23, May 17, 18, 21, August 2, 3, 1853).

Two letters giving a detailed account by Finn of the Artas
case, mentioning departure of the American group to settle at Jaffa
some months before, and the subsequent attempt of Mr. Jones and
Mary Williams to regain possession of property at Artas (File 445/
January 28, 31, 1854).

List of U.S. agents in Palestine in 1854: Saida: Vice Consul,
Ibrahim Nakhly; Soor (Tyre): Vice Consul, Yakoob Akal; Acre:
Vice Consul, Girges Gemmal; Caiffa (Haifa): Vice Consul, G. A.
Nasrallah; Jaffa: Vice Consul, Yakoob Serapion; Jerusalem: agent,
Simon Serapion, depending on Jaffa; Ramlah: agent, Nicola abud
Murkos, depending on Jaffa; and Nazareth: agent, name unknown,
depending on Acre. "Everyone of these eight persons is a native of

the country and unpaid. And everyone has a train of dependents. . . . Everyone has a flag, except the agents in Jerusalem and Nazareth" (File 445/August 17, 1854).

Handlist of volumes available in repository.

Published index *Records of the Foreign Office, PRO Handbook No. 13.*

Research access not restricted. Photocopies provided.

VL 7/82

GREAT BRITAIN, FOREIGN OFFICE (FO), GENERAL COR-RESPONDENCE, TURKISH EMPIRE TO 1905
(Some 140 of the 5,490 volumes contain correspondence and other papers from Jerusalem and other consulates in Eretz Israel 1838-1905; complemented by FO 195.)
450 pages and 22 items, covering years 1853, 1855-1857, 1866, 1868, 1900-1901, in ten volumes, interspersed in Record Group FO 78—selected themes.

In Public Record Office, Kew Gardens, London.

Collection includes consular despatches (1853-1857) regarding U.S. Millerite settlers, including Clorinda Minor, on the farm of John Meshullam at Artas in 1852 and the involvement of British Consul James Finn in the Minor-Meshullam dispute, British jurisdiction over Mary Williams and charges of dishonesty against Finn's dragoman, Moussa Tannous, by American missionary James T. Barclay regarding land purchase at Wady Farah (Files 962, 963, 1138, 1218, 1295); and arrival and subsequent difficulties of the Adams colonists in Jaffa in 1866 and later efforts by George Jones Adams to reach England and encourage English people to revive the colony in 1868 (Files 1929; 2048); U.S. consular activities of the Kayat family: H. A. Kayat, Vice Consul in Jaffa in 1866 (File 1929), William Henry Kayat, unpaid Pro Consul in Jerusalem in 1901, native of Syria, a naturalized U.S. citizen and the subject of charges by Anglican Bishop Blyth (Files 5139; 5470).

Other U.S. consular representatives figuring in the collection include J. Hosford Smith (Files 962; 963; 1138), Henry Wood (Files 1138; 1218), Selah Merrill as regards Miss Hussey and Captain Johnson (File 5470); see also St. Anthony's Middle East Centre, Dickson Papers).

Of special interest:

Despatch (February 9, 1853) from Consul Finn, enclosing correspondence with U.S. Consul J. Hosford Smith, about Miss Mary Williams, an English lady who had joined the U.S. Millerite settlers at Artas in 1852 and requested and received the protection of the U.S. Consul despite protests by Finn (File 962).

Despatch (February 26, 1853) containing a detailed account by Finn of the Artas affair: history of John Meshullam, who in 1849 was keeping a Jerusalem hotel at which two American "fanatics or worse, then called Mr. and Mrs. Adams" stayed; their visit to the Meshullam farm at Artas and subsequent return to Philadelphia to collect funds for the settlement; reappearance of Miss Adams as Mrs. Clorinda Minor with her son and 20 settlers at Artas in March 1852; agreement on joint cultivation with Meshullam dissolved by him "because of certain immoralities of Mrs. Minor under the name of religion"; American appeal to Consul Smith who began enquiry at Artas with Finn in February, 1853, but left before its completion; refusal of Americans to give up property. Enclosures include memo (February 22, 1853) by Cyrus Thatcher on behalf of Mrs. Minor; notes on unfinished inquiry; contract with Americans signed on behalf of Meshullam (May 14, 1852); FO minute on despatch: "What has FO to do with this matter? It is a private contract squabble" (File 963).

Entire 450-page volume (January-May 1855) of Lord Napier's report on charges brought by the U.S. Consul at Beirut against Consul Finn including complaints of his discourtesy to U.S. consular officers, his involvement in the Meshullam-Minor dispute at Artas, his conduct in relation to his dragoman, negotiations by Moussa Tannous concerning U.S. missionary James T. Barclay, arrangement with U.S. Minister to Turkey Carroll Spence for attendance of U.S. Consul Henry Wood at inquiry in Jerusalem; 30-page summary report; 115-page final report; 290 pages of appendixes, mainly copies of correspondence and notes of evidence; record of despatch of report with original copy of U.S. memorandum on complaint (see Great Britain, FO 5/606); despatch of Foreign Secretary (May 17, 1855) approving proceedings by Napier (File 1138).

Report (September 26, 1866) by H. A. Kayat, recently appointed Vice Consul at Jaffa to succeed his deceased father, describing the arrival of 156 Adams colonists on the U.S. clipper *Nelly*

Chapin; their pitching tents temporarily, purposely to move "in a few days . . . to a plot of land outside the town, which was purchased for them some months ago from Mr. Loewenthal, the United States vice-consul here"; their "strong and earnest desire to live and die in the Holy Land," to cultivate the land, to set a good example in agriculture and trades, to live peaceably and to submit to all local regulations; Adams as energetic and enthusiastic; local authorities making no difficulties at their landing (File 1929).

Despatch covering Kayat report of September 26, 1866, from Noel Temple Moore, Consul at Jerusalem, stating he had encouraged Izzet Pasha to extend colonists a friendly reception and afford them facilities and protection; describing subsequent difficulties of the enterprise and problems arising from failure of the colonists to fulfil regulations regarding foreign colonization in Turkey (File 1929).

Despatch (July 2, 1868) to FO from Consul Temple Moore, describing Adams' departure after the demise of the American colony at Jaffa and his intentions of proceeding to England to induce English people to come to Jaffa and revive the colony; negative evaluation of Adams, questioning his fitness to manage such a scheme; failure of the American settlement at Jaffa but a repetition of the fate of previous similar experiments under better auspices. "In present circumstances, both as regards the country itself, and the still unsettled question of land tenure by foreign subjects in Turkey. . . . There seems little hope of success attending these enterprises. . . ." (File 2048).

Chronological registers of contents of General Correspondence of FO available in FO 802 in repository.

Published index *Records of the Foreign Office*, *PRO Handbook No. 13*.

Research access not restricted. Photocopies provided.

VL 7/82

GREAT BRITAIN, FOREIGN OFFICE (FO), GENERAL COR-RESPONDENCE, UNITED STATES TO 1906

11 items, covering years 1853-1855, interspersed in Record Group FO 5.

In Public Record Office, Kew Gardens, London.

Of special interest in the collection are the following documents relating to the alleged improper conduct of British Consul James

Finn toward U.S. Vice Consul S. S. Murad and other U.S. nationals in Jerusalem in 1854-1855:

Detailed statement (received in FO, January 24, 1855) from U.S. Secretary of State William Marcy to Ambassador Buchanan on the conduct of Finn and request for explanation, including Marcy's letter of October 26, 1854; report by J. Hosford Smith, "late Consul at Beyrout" (June 5, 1854) mentioning J. Murad appointed first United States Vice Consul for Jerusalem in April 1852 with a testimonial to his character (June 1853) signed by G. B. Whitney, E. G. Smith, W. M. Thomson, Henry A. de Forest, S. H. Calhoun, George C. Hurter; record of proceedings before the British consular court in Jerusalem (March 15, 1853) in the case of James Barclay; statement by Stephen W. Jones, "agent for the American Citizens" (File 606—Incoming Correspondence, 1855, pp. 320-367).

Correspondence in June-July 1855 between Foreign Secretary Lord Clarendon and Ambassador Buchanan regarding the report by Lord Napier on the complaints against Finn and the divergent report of Consul Henry Wood to Marcy; minute signed "C" (Lord Clarendon): "What are we to do about this? I suppose a reproof of Mr. Finn and a caution not to interfere in matters that do not concern him will suffice" (File 632).

Draft letter (August 10, 1855) to Consul Finn from Lord Clarendon reprimanding him for his conduct, exhorting him to maintain friendly relations with the authorities of the United States and mentioning the legal case respecting the litigated property at Artas in the Clorinda Minor-John Meshullam dispute; accompanying minute by Permanent Under Secretary E. B. Hammond, deploring the matter and its triviality; minute (August 9, 1855) by Lord Clarendon requesting copies of the draft be sent to Lord Stratford de Redcliffe (Ambassador at Constantinople) and approving the "judgement, impartiality and perspicacity with which Lord Napier conducted the enquiry" and to Mr. Crampton (chargé d'affaires in Washington) for communication to Secretary of State William Marcy (File 1120—General Correspondence with United States, August 1855).

Registers of contents of FO General Correspondence available in FO 802 at the repository.

Research access not restricted. Photocopies provided.

VL 7/82

GREAT BRITAIN, FOREIGN OFFICE (FO), GENERAL POLIT-
ICAL CORRESPONDENCE
(Correspondence with FO beginning with year 1906.)
Over 300 items, covering specimen years 1917-1920, 1922-1925,
1927-1930 with references back to 1914, interspersed in Record
Group 371—selected themes, excluding material already published.
In Public Record Office, Kew Gardens, London.

Collection includes copies of despatches, letters, cables and
minutes concerning the following British FO and Colonial Office
(CO), U.S. State Department and Government associates and Jewish
personalities involved in Palestine, frequently referred to by last
name only below (positions and titles cited below refer to date of
document quoted):

BRITISH FO AND CO OFFICIALS

Balfour, Arthur James, Earl of—Foreign Secretary, 1916-1919
Barclay, Colville—counsellor, Washington Embassy
Bennett, Courtney—Consul General, New York, 1914
Bentwich, Norman—Legal Secretary (later Attorney General)
of Palestine Government
Cecil, Lord Robert—Parliamentary Under Secretary of State for
Foreign Affairs 1916-1919
Chamberlain, Austen—Foreign Secretary, 1924-1929
Churchill, Winston—Secretary of War and Air, 1919-1921;
Under Secretary for the Colonies, 1921-1922
Clayton, Gilbert (Brigadier General)—Chief Political Officer,
Egyptian Expeditionary Force, 1917-1919
Crowe, Sir Eyre—Assistant Under Secretary of State for Foreign
Affairs, 1920-1925
Curzon, Lord (George Nathaniel)—Foreign Secretary, 1919-
1924
Drummond, Sir Eric—private secretary to Foreign Secretary,
1915-1919
Fullerton Carnegie, G. O. H.—Third Secretary, Eastern Depart-
ment
Geddes, Sir Auckland—Ambassador, Washington, 1920-1924
Graham, Ronald—Assistant Under Secretary of State, 1916-
1919
Hardinge, Lord—Permanent Under Secretary of State, 1916-
1920

Henderson, Arthur—Secretary of State for Foreign Affairs, 1929-1931

Howard, Sir Esmé—Ambassador, Washington, 1929

Kidston, G. J.—First Secretary, Eastern Department, FO, 1920

Lindsay, Sir Ronald—Permanent Under Secretary, FO, 1928-1930; Ambassador, Washington, 1930-1939

Lloyd George, David—Prime Minister, 1916-1922

Oliphant, Lancelot—Counsellor, FO, 1921-1928

(Ormsby Gore, W.), Lord Harlech—Member of Parliament from 1910, Assistant Secretary of Cabinet, 1917-1918

Percy, Lord Eustace—accompanied Balfour to United States in 1917, later Lord Percy of Newcastle

Rendel, George—FO official, 1929

Shuckburgh, Sir John Evelyn—India Office, 1920; head of Middle East Department, CO, 1921-1931

Spring Rice, Sir Cecil—Ambassador, Washington, 1913-1918

Toynbee, Arnold Joseph—FO Political Intelligence Department, 1917-1918

Williams, O. G. R.—Assistant Secretary, CO, 1926-1946

Wingate, Sir Reginald—High Commissioner, Egypt, 1917-1919

Young, Hubert—Assistant Secretary, CO, 1921-1927

U.S. EMISSARIES OR STATE DEPARTMENT OFFICIALS

Crane, Charles—Chicago businessman with many connections in Near East, member of the King-Crane Commission (1919)

Dawes, Charles—Ambassador, London, 1929-1931

Dulles, Allen—head of Near East Department, 1922-1926

Edelman, Samuel—Vice Consul in Berne, Switzerland, 1917

House, Edward (Colonel)—special adviser to President Wilson 1914-1919

Kellogg, Frank B.—Ambassador, London, 1924-1925

Lansing, Robert—Secretary of State, 1915-1920

Morgenthau, Henry, Sr.—Ambassador to Turkey, 1913-1916

Murray, Wallace—head of Near Eastern Division of State Department

Page, Walter—Ambassador, London, 1913-1918

Polk, Frank—Counsellor, State Department (1915-1919)

Yale, William—agent of Standard Oil, then special U.S. intelligence agent in the Near East during and after World War I

JEWISH PERSONALITIES

Aaronsohn, Aaron—agronimist and Zionist activist
Brandeis, Louis D.—Justice, U.S. Supreme Court and American Zionist leader
Frankfurter, Felix—Justice, U.S. Supreme Court
Namier, Lewis Bernstein—(FO Research Department) British historian and Zionist ideologue
Schiff, Jacob—financier and philanthropist
Weizmann, Chaim—first President of the State of Israel and distinguished scientist
Wise, Stephen S.—rabbi and American Zionist leader

Material in the collection involves the following aspects of Anglo-American relations concerning Palestine:

Foreign Office pressure to allow sending the American Zionist Medical Unit to Palestine (File 3057/May 30 and July 20, 1918).

Standard Oil Company concessions and geological report in Palestine in 1914: action by the British Government to prevent Standard Oil from acquiring oil concessions from Suleiman Bey Nassif. Personalities and/or companies mentioned include Courtney Bennett, Lord Cowdray of S. Pearson and Co., Suleiman Bey Nassif, geological adviser G. S. Blake and the Turkish Petroleum Company (Files 2124, 12279, 10090/March 17 and June 24, 1914).

Proposed 1917 mission of Henry Morgenthau, Sr., to Turkey to test the possibility of a separate peace with the Allies, under cover of a visit concerned with aid to the Jewish community in Palestine; assessment of Morgenthau's appropriateness for the mission and his alleged connection with Turkish secret Shabbetaians (remnants of the sect believing Shabbetai Zevi a messiah); meeting between Chaim Weizmann and Morgenthau at Gibraltar. Personalities mentioned include Robert Lansing, Lancelot Oliphant, Ronald Graham, Cecil Spring Rice, Jacob Schiff, Felix Frankfurter, Lord Balfour, Colville Barclay and Frank Polk (Files 3055 and 3017/May-July, 1917).

Possible involvement of the United States in the future administration of Palestine; Louis D. Brandeis advocating a British protectorate in preference to American involvement; Lord Balfour preferring association of the United States in the protectorate. Personalities mentioned include Eric Drummond, Lord Balfour, David Lloyd

George, Louis D. Brandeis, Walter Page and Robert Cecil (File 3035/ April 24, 1917; File 3058/June 12, 1917; File 3061/December 20, 1917; File 4181/June 26, 1919).

Anti-Zionist report by Samuel Edelman, U.S. Vice Consul in Berne, dated December 3, 1917, stating that American interests in Palestine were negligible with reference to a "secret agreement" with the Vatican for Catholic support in return for Jewish influence in favor of Vatican representation at the Peace Conference; comments by Arnold Toynbee, Lewis B. Namier, Ronald Graham and Chaim Weizmann (File 3054/December 19, 1917).

British Government fear that relations with U.S. Zionists after the Balfour Declaration would alienate the U.S. Government and populace. Personalities include Spring Rice, Lansing, Graham, Colonel Edward House, Stephen S. Wise, Lord Percy, Robert Cecil, Jacob Schiff and Lord Hardinge (Files 3054 and 3055/December 19 and 28, 1919).

William Yale, secret agent, and his machinations in connection with Standard Oil and the King-Crane Commission. Personalities mentioned include Brigadier General Buckley, W. Ormsby Gore, Hudson Geary, G. J. Kidston, Lord Curzon, Ronald Graham and John Shuckburgh (File 3057/July 16, 1917; File 3417/November 20, 1918; File 4081/June 13, 1919).

Zionist Organization of America (ZOA) sending a delegation in 1922 to British Ambassador in Washington, Auckland Geddes to express the anxieties of American Zionists about rumors of unrest in Palestine (File 7773/March 9, April 11 and 14, 1922).

Role of Zionist efforts in passage of the Joint Congressional Resolution on Palestine, June 30, 1922. Personalities mentioned include G. Fullerton Carnegie and Nahum Sokolow (Files 7773 and 7774/July 4, 1922).

Anglo-American Convention of 1924 on rights of U.S. Government in Palestine; details of the negotiations leading to signature of the convention on December 2, 1924 and exchange of ratifications on December 3, 1925; jurisdiction of Palestine courts over U.S. nationals. Persons and court cases mentioned in the files include Austen Chamberlain, Frank B. Kellog, Colonel Stirling (Counsellor at U.S. Embassy, London), Allan Dulles, Lancelot Oliphant, Cecil Spring Rice, Hubert Young, Elimelech Sachs, Pacovsky v. Philip Skora, Tel Aviv Municipality v. Israel Hanovice, Eva Zimmerman

v. Max Bension, Anglo-Egyptian Bank v. Texas Co., Pelner v. Golding, J. Zaslavski v. Tobia Goldberg, Zipora Bat Zion v. Mrs. Louis Feynman, Abraham Weinberg v. Israel Dodd Lyon alias Bernard Levine, Dov Toubkin v. Meyer Shapiro, Zvi Weiman v. Abraham Beitner (Files 9012, 10835, 12279).

Reactions of U.S. Government to 1929 riots, including requests for protection of American life and property and possibility of despatching the U.S.S. *Raleigh* and U.S.S. *Trenton* to Palestine. Persons mentioned include G. R. Williams, George Rendel, Second Secretary Cox (U.S. Embassy, London), Lancelot Oliphant, Charles Dawes, Ronald Lindsay, John Chancellor, Esmé Howard and Senator William Borah of Idaho (Files 13751 and 13752, especially Folder E4348/August 27-September 9, 1929).

Reactions in the United States to the Hope-Simpson Report and Passfield White Paper: hostility of the American Jewish press; fairness of the general press; sympathy of the U.S. Government. Persons mentioned include Daniel Hopkins, President Herbert Hoover and Wallace Murray (File 14491).

Healing of the Brandeis-Lipsky dispute in American Zionism (File 14491/Ambassador's report, July 12, 1930).

United States Government requesting special privileges for foreign career consular officers in mandated territories; CO asked by FO to attempt accommodation along lines already conceded by France in Syria (Files 14492/E2479, May 1930); and negative influence on American Jews of an article by Winston Churchill in *America* on November 2, 1930 (File 14494/November 6, 1930); correspondence between Ronald Lindsay and Arthur Henderson (File 14491).

Of special interest in the collection are the following documents:

A cable (June 9, 1917) from Spring Rice stating that Henry Morgenthau, Sr., was pro-German, closely connected with Turkish Jews and "Dunmeis" (sic, that is, Dönmeh, secret followers of Shabbetai Zevi known to be in Salonica) and influential among the Young Turks (File 3017).

Cables (June 12 and 19, 1917) from Spring Rice stating that Morgenthau would be accompanied by Felix Frankfurter and that the State Department wished Weizmann to meet Morgenthau in hopes that the credit of the mission would be increased by the presence of Frankfurter, "who is a real Jew. . . ." (File 3017).

Minutes by Eric Drummond of an interview held April 24, 1917 with Brandeis and of a subsequent Balfour-Brandeis meeting, when Brandeis advocated a British protectorate in preference to American involvement (File 3035).

A cable (December 28, 1917) from Spring Rice about a discussion with Robert Lansing and Colonel Edward House about Zionists in America and the possibility that too intimate relations with them would alienate the opposing faction; Catholics pressing claims in Jerusalem; inability of the United States, not at war with Turkey, to take part in dividing up Turkish territory and of the British Ambassador to support U.S. citizens with that objective; importance of maintaining "good and friendly relations with Zionists and U.S. Government hopes that Jews' influence may be exercised for good in Russia" (File 3054).

Reports (June 20 and July 16, 1917) attesting that before becoming a secret agent for the United States in the Near East, William Yale tried unsuccessfully to become a British agent (File 3057).

A warning (June 13, 1919) by G. J. Kidston to newly appointed Foreign Secretary Lord Curzon that Yale, attached to the King-Crane Commission, had Standard Oil connections, that "his presence may prove highly awkward and that this gentleman's activities will need careful watching" (File 4081).

A despatch (December 30, 1930) from the British Ambassador in Washington, Ronald Lindsay, analyzing American attitudes to Zionism and sensing a coming pressure for change in American policy as regards Palestine as well as deploring the unwillingness of the State Department to face this prospect (File 14491).

Card index of subjects, places and persons available in repository.

Published *Records of the Foreign Office* (*PRO Handbook No. 13*).

Research access not restricted. Photocopies provided.

Microfilm at Israel State Archives, Jerusalem in Record Group 123/2.

VL 8/82

GREAT BRITAIN, FOREIGN OFFICE (FO), NEWS DEPARTMENT
(From 1914-1918 operated as propaganda department; after 1917 functioned in association with Ministry of Information.)

1 item of 4 pages, dated 1918, in Record Group FO 395/245.
In Public Record Office, Kew Gardens, London.

Item no. 117084 of the file consists of a cover letter (July 1, 1918) to Stephen Gaselee, head of the News Department, from Albert Hyamson, then head of the Jewish Section of the Ministry of Information applying for permission to publish the text of the congratulatory address by Foreign Secretary Lord Balfour to the American Zionist Medical Unit on its way to Palestine. Also included are the text of the speech; the comment by Balfour: "Need we publish this balderdash?," interpreted by his secretary, Sir Eric Drummond, as authority to release the statement through Zionists to the Anglo-Jewish and American-Jewish Press; Gaselee's reaction (July 9, 1918) to Balfour's comment on his own words: "the self-deprecating feeling of the great.".
Card index of subjects, places and persons available in repository.
Published index to *Records of the Foreign Office* (*PRO Handbook No. 13*).
Research access not restricted. Photocopies provided.

VL 8/82

GREAT BRITAIN, STATE PAPERS FOREIGN, ARCHIVES OF BRITISH LEGATIONS
4 items, covering years 1823-1824, in Record Group SP 105.
In Public Record Office (PRO), Chancery Lane, London.

Items consist of letters regarding the activities of Pliny Fisk and Jonas King; protests against a firman banning the distribution of English Bibles by American missionaries (out-letters 124; 125 and in-letters 141; 142/p.234).

Of special interest are: a letter (September 28, 1824) to John Barker, Consul at Aleppo, signed by Pliny Fisk, Jonas King, British Foreign Bible Society agent Benjamin Barker and clergyman William B. Lewis, requesting permission to resume Bible distributions which had been prohibited by a firman from Constantinople; and a reply (October 4, 1824) by Consul Barker that he had forwarded their letter to his superiors in Constantinople for consideration as a question of both political and religious interest (File SP 105/142, pp. 239, 240).
Handlist of files available in repository.
Research access not restricted. Photocopies provided.

VL 7/82

GREAT BRITAIN, WAR CABINET AND CABINET, MINUTES
Ca. 20 items, covering years 1916-1921, interspersed in Record
Group CAB 23/Files 1-44.
In Public Record Office (PRO), Kew Gardens, London.
Of special interest among the occasional references to American
involvement in Palestine are the following items from the meetings
held just prior to the approval of the Balfour Declaration:

> a statement (September 3, 1917) by acting Foreign Secretary
> Lord Robert Cecil regarding the potential value to the Allies of
> having the support of the"strong and enthusiastic organization,
> more particularly in the United States, who were zealous in
> this [Zionism] " (War Cabinet Minute W.C. 227/2);
> a statement (October 4, 1917) by Lord Balfour as Foreign
> Secretary that the Zionist movement had "the support of a
> majority of Jews in Russia and America. . . . He knew that
> President Wilson was extremely favourable to the movement";
> attention was drawn to contradictory telegrams from Colonel
> Edward House and Justice Brandeis about the attitude of the
> United States Government; a decision made by the War Cabinet
> that the formula of the declaration as submitted by Lord Milner
> should be referred to President Wilson, among others (War Cabi-
> net Minute W.C. 245/18); and
> a statement by Balfour at the meeting (October 31, 1917) at
> which the final text of the Balfour Declaration was approved:
> "the vast majority of Jews in . . . America . . . now appeared to
> be favourable to Zionism" (War Cabinet Minute W.C. 261/
> afternoon session).

Of special interest also is the cabinet minute (May 31, 1921)
recording resistance by Winston Churchill, then Secretary of State
for the Colonies and responsible for administration of Palestine, to
the proposal that application to the League of Nations for approval
of granting the Palestine mandate to Britain should be postponed
because of American opposition; view was approved by the Cabinet
and commended to Foreign Secretary Lord Curzon and H. A. L.
Fisher, president of the Board of Education, who would be British
representatives at the next League of Nations meeting (CAB 23/25,
Cabinet Conclusions, 45(21), 2(a)).

Minutes of the War Cabinet and Cabinet can be understood only with reference to the series of memoranda papers which were circulated before and discussed at the meetings.

Subject index in repository. Index to conclusions found in *The Records of the Cabinet Office to 1922* (*PRO Handbook No. 11*).

Research access not restricted. Photocopies provided.

Complete photographic copy on open shelves in repository.

VL 7/82

GREAT BRITAIN, WAR CABINET AND CABINET, REGISTERED FILES

Ca. 10 items, covering years 1916-1922, interspersed in Record Group CAB 21.

In Public Record Office (PRO), Kew Gardens, London.

File 58 (originally numbered 18/0A/5, headed "Zionism") contains the originals of such documents as the telegram from Louis D. Brandeis to Chaim Weizmann (September 26, 1917) stating that President Woodrow Wilson's "entire sympathy" was with the proposed Balfour Declaration.

Of special interest is a letter (October 31, 1918) from W. G. A. Ormsby Gore in Palestine to Sir Eyre Crowe, then Assistant Under Secretary of State at FO, quoting a letter from an American Zionist in New York who had been with Ormsby Gore in Palestine: "The idea that the United States should be charged with the task of governing or administering Palestine . . . does not obtain here [i.e. in New York]. I rather fear the possibility of opposition in the United States to a British Trusteeship of Palestine more from military sources than from any other."

Collection catalogued by repository.

Research access not restricted. Photocopies provided.

VL 7/82

GROSSMAN, MEIR, 1888-1964

(Born in Russia; journalist and Zionist Revisionist leader; founded *Jerusalem Bulletin*, later the *Palestine Post* then *Jerusalem Post*.)

Ca. 187 items, covering years 1920, 1927-1939, 1942, interspersed in Record Group P 59.

In Jabotinsky Institute in Israel, Tel Aviv.

Collection includes correspondence and minutes of meetings regarding Revisionist activity in the United States and includes the following:

Relations between Revisionists and other Zionist groups, e.g., Poalei Zion, Hadassah, Mizrachi, ZOA, its leadership and the opposing group led by Louis D. Brandeis, reflected in Grossman's correspondence with Elias Gilner (Ginsburg), Jacob De Haas, Mordecai Danzis, Abraham Tulin and Johan Smertenko (Folders 2/13; 2/57; 2/90/14; 2/91/4; 2/92/2; 2/93/7; 2/96/2; 2/102/8).

Activities of the Jewish State Party in the United States and its supporters Israel Baratz, Meir Chuchem and Sol Liptzin (Folders 2/36; 2/89/25; 2/95/1; 2/99/10).

Anti-partitionist activities among Revisionists, Hadassah and such Jewish leaders as Robert Szold, Julian Mack and Abba Hillel Silver (Folders 2/36; 2/62; 2/100/2; 2/102/1; 2/102/4).

Speaking tours by Grossman in the United States and his articles circulated by United Press Association, *Der Tog*, *The Jewish Tribune* and *Menorah Journal* (Folders 2/55,57; 2/75; 2/87; 2/91/9).

Financial support by Judge Henry Dannenbaum of Texas for the Revisionist movement and his sympathy with the policies of Jabotinsky (Folders 2/91/3).

Statements by Israel Brodie in 1937-1939 that Eretz Israel is economically capable of supporting a large population and that chastise doubting Jewish leaders who "grasp at every silly scheme" proposed by the British Government for colonization elsewhere (Folder 2/89/17).

Of special interest are the following:

a letter to Grossman from Israel Baratz (February 1, 1935), expressing vehement objections to Jabotinsky and predicting the failure of his forthcoming tour in the United States because "American Zionists do not favor breaking the Zionist Organization, nor are they willing to follow blindly the 'Fuerer' (sic)" (Folder 2/89/25); and

letter dated April 18, 1928 from Grossman to Stephen S. Wise suggesting that Wise join forces with the Revisionists against the policy of Chaim Weizmann and assume leadership of the movement; response by Wise dated May 3, 1928 that he can be of much greater service without joining forces with Jabotinsky (Folder 2/93/7).

Collection catalogued by repository.
Research access not restricted. Photocopies provided.

TG 12/81

GRUENWALD, KURT, 1901-1975
(Banker, economist, public figure in Jerusalem.)
1 item, dated 1936, in Record Group A 343.
In Central Zionist Archives, Jerusalem.

A 3-page confidential memorandum by Gruenwald dated July 8, 1936 describes the political situation in Palestine, particularly the riots of 1936; negotiations between Mussa Effendi Alami and a Jewish group which included Judah L. Magnes and Maurice Hexter; and American financing of Arab riots: ". . . it seems to be certain that considerable amounts have come from the USA be it from Arabs over there, be it from Crane and his friends through his local agent, Mr. Antonius" (Folder 4).
Collection catalogued by repository.
Research access not restricted. Photocopies provided.

ML 2/81

HABIMAH THEATER
(Repertory theater company founded in Moscow in 1917 by Nahum David Zemach; settled in Eretz Israel in 1931.)
1 item, dated 1926, in the special Habimah collection.
In Theater Archives, Tel Aviv University, Tel Aviv.

Item is a contract and auxiliary agreement dated July 23, 1926 in Russian and English between the manager of Habimah, Nahum David Zemach, and impresario Sol Hurok of New York for a tour of the Habimah Theater Company in the United States and Canada from November 22, 1926 through February 25, 1927.
Collection uncatalogued. Name of collection temporary.
Access by permission of archivist. Photocopies not provided.

TG 5/81

HACOHEN, MORDECHAI BEN HILLEL, 1856-1936
(Born in Byelorussia; Hebrew writer and Zionist; settled in Eretz Israel in 1907; among the founders of Tel Aviv.)
1 item, dated 1927, in Record Group 4° 1068.
In Jewish National and University Library, Jerusalem.

Item is a letter concerning the visit of Jacob Schiff to Eretz Israel during that year (Folder 28).

Collection catalogued by repository.

Research access not restricted. Photocopies provided.

SK 4/82

HAFFKINE, WALDEMAR MORDECAI, 1860-1930

(Born in Odessa; internationally known bacteriologist; settled in France; active Zionist.)

21 items, covering years 1917, 1922-1926, in Record Group Ms. Var. 325.

In Jewish National and University Library, Jerusalem.

Collection includes handwritten notes and typewritten minutes of the meeting between Haffkine and United States Ambassador to Turkey, Abram Issac Elkus, reflecting the Ambassador's familiarity with the Zionist aspirations and plight of the Jews in Eretz Israel as well as efforts by Louis D. Brandeis to keep Woodrow Wilson informed of these matters (File 259).

Also includes correspondence and diary entries in French and English concerning the establishment of the Institute of Jewish Studies at the Hebrew University, for which funds were donated by Solomon Rosenbloom who, together with Haffkine, favored an Orthodox approach for the school in contrast to the more liberal attitude of Judah L. Magnes. Besides Haffkine, correspondents include Solomon Rosenbloom, Cyrus Adler, Eliezer Ben Yehuda and Joseph H. Hertz (Chief Rabbi of the British Empire). Other Americans featured in the correspondence include Judah L. Magnes, Louis D. Brandeis, Julian Mack, Felix Warburg, Louis Ginzberg and Max L. Margolis.

Of special interest is a copy of a 2-page letter dated 1922 from Rosenbloom to Ben Yehuda stating the need for the proposed Institute of Jewish Studies as a bulwark against assimilation and erosion of Jewish values and mentioning that Judges Brandeis and Mack support this view (File 228).

Collection catalogued by repository.

Research access not restricted. Photocopies provided.

SK 3/82

HAKIBBUTZ HAMEUHAD, COMMITTEE FOR ACTIVITIES ABROAD

(Union of kibbutzim in Eretz Israel founded at a conference in Petah Tikvah in 1924.)
38 items, covering years 1930-1948, in Record Group 2.
In Hakibbutz Hameuhad Archives, Ramat Efal, Ramat Gan.

Collection, mainly in Hebrew, includes two letters dated 1937 to Israel Idelson (Bar Yehuda) from Benzion Apelboim (Ilan) and Enzo Sereni, respectively, attributing the difficulties of American immigrants at kibbutzim to the transition from American individualism to kibbutz collectivism as a way of life (Folder 98).

Collection also includes minutes of meetings and correspondence with emissaries of Hakibbutz Hameuhad on the following subjects: their activities in American Jewish communities (Folders 19; 24; 98); the need for more Yiddish and English-speaking emissaries; Americans desiring to join kibbutzim; reactions to American positions regarding creation of the State of Israel in March through May, 1948; the merger of Ahdut Ha'avoda and American Poalei Zion parties in 1947; the floundering state of the Hechalutz movement in the United States during 1937-1939. Among the correspondents are Golda Myerson (Meir), Yitzhak Ben Aharon and Yehiel Shemi (Folder 98).

Folder 98 of the collection contains 2 letters requesting that kibbutz publications be sent to the newly established library archive of the United Jewish Socialist Poalei Zion-Zeirei Zion Party of America, in a letter from Rafael Margolin dated April 7, 1932; and to the Hechalutz Organization in America because members are eager for more information about the kibbutz, in a letter from secretary Nahum Gutman dated January 10, 1938.
Collection catalogued by repository.
Research access not restricted. Photocopies provided.

TG 9/81

HAKIBBUTZ HAMEUHAD, COUNCILS

2 items, dated 1939 and 1944, in Record Group 5.
In Hakibbutz Hameuhad Archives, Ramat Efal, Ramat Gan.

Folders 2 and 3 each contain a letter in Hebrew discussing the situation of the movement and its emissaries in the United States and

describing American youth as knowing very little about either Judaism or Zionism.
Collection catalogued by repository.
Research access not restricted. Photocopies provided.

TG 10/81

HAKIBBUTZ HAMEUHAD, IMMIGRATION AND ABSORPTION COMMITTEE
5 items, covering years 1934-1936, in Record Group 2.
In Hakibbutz Hameuhad Archives, Ramat Efal, Ramat Gan.

Items consist of applications and letters in Hebrew from Americans requesting to join or change kibbutzim (Folders 1 and 3), and a list of immigrants at the Anglo-Baltic kibbutz (later Kfar Blum) of whom three were Americans (Folder 2).
Collection catalogued by repository.
Research access not restricted. Photocopies provided.

TG 8/81

HAKIBBUTZ HAMEUHAD, SECRETARIAT
39 items, covering years 1928-1948, interspersed in Record Groups 1A (correspondence) and 1B (minutes).
In Hakibbutz Hameuhad Archives, Ramat Efal, Ramat Gan.

Collection contains the following material relating to Americans who joined kibbutzim in the early 1930s: correspondence, mainly in Hebrew, pertaining to arrangements for groups of American settlers and their absorption at kibbutzim Ein Harod, Kinneret, Deganya and Naan (Folders 1A/13,21,27,41,100); and two letters requesting placement at kibbutzim for individuals in New York (Yiddish) and Cleveland (Hebrew from Abraham Regelson, mentioning Golda Myerson (Meir) as one of his references).

Also included are brief reports in Hebrew about placement of American immigrants in various kibbutzim and other settlements: suggestions for placing groups of American settlers in Givat Hasheloshah, Gesher, Yagur, Rishon Lezion and Ramat David (Books 1B/21 and 5); and an objection in 1940 to the Anglo-Baltic kibbutz (later Kfar Blum) accepting a group of Americans without previously consulting with, and securing the agreement of, the secretariat of Hakibbutz Hameuhad (Folder 1B/24).

Also includes correspondence and memoranda (mainly in Hebrew) regarding activities of emissaries of Hakibbutz Hameuhad to the United States especially with Pioneer Women and Habonim (Folders 1A/84,100,102). Subjects include the following:

Completion in 1943 of the Pioneer Women House in Jerusalem, despite considerable difficulties, and the forwarding of more funds by the Women's League for Israel towards construction of similar houses in Tel Aviv and Haifa (Folder 1A/84).

Pioneer Women fundraising in 1942 and 1943 for youth institutions in Eretz Israel objected to by Hadassah as infringing on its exclusive role in Youth Aliyah (Folder 1A/84).

Suggestion in 1929 that the management of *Davar* publish a weekly edition of the newspaper in English for distribution in America to provide accurate facts about the 1929 riots and thus counter misinformation disseminated by unfriendly sources (Folder 1A/12).

Information supplied to Pioneer Women in America in 1931 about terms for accepting members in Hakibbutz Hameuhad (Folder 1A/26).

Hebrew translation of a speech delivered by Robert Szold at a joint session of the committees of the Zionist Organization of America and Hadassah on October 17, 1942, in which he reaffirmed and explained the Biltmore Program (Folder 1A/86).

Decision in 1928 to send Yehudit Simhoni to America and discussions with Israel Mereminsky about organizing an American campaign to purchase land in Eretz Israel (Book 1B/2).

Demand by Rahel Katznelson, before leaving for the United States as an emissary of Moetzet Hapoalot (Council of Women Workers), that more kibbutz emissaries be sent; comment by Yitzhak Tabenkin that Americans usually find adjustment to kibbutz life more difficult because they lack pioneer spirit and drive for self-fulfillment (Folder 1B/10A).

Activities of the Labor Zionist and kibbutz movement in America during 1938-1939, 1946-1947 in brief reports by Yehudit Simhoni, Enzo Sereni, Yitzhak Ben Aharon and other emissaries (Books 1B/18,19, 20, 33).

Collection catalogued by repository.

Research access not restricted. Photocopies provided.

TG 6/81

HAMIZRACHI-HOVEVEI ZION IN RUSSIA

(Founded in 1893 in response to request of Rabbi Samuel Mohilewer to establish a spiritual center for Hovevei Zion movement.)
12 items, covering years 1893-1901, in Record Group V. 709.
In Jewish National and University Library, Jerusalem.

Collection includes correspondence in Hebrew between Adam Rosenberg, member of New York Hovevei Zion, and Rabbi Samuel Mohilewer, regarding the establishment of a Hovevei Zion settlement in the Golan Heights; difficulties in raising money for the proposed settlement; Turkish restrictions on purchasing land; and disagreement with the American Hovevei Zion movement concerning the project (Folders 21; 195).

Of special interest is a 2-page letter (10 Sivan 5654 [1894]) in Hebrew from Adam Rosenberg to Hamizrachi enumerating the problems besetting the purchase of land for the settlement, while citing the readiness of 200 members of the American and British Hovevei Zion organizations and Agudat Shaarei Zion to settle on the new *moshava* (Folder 195).

The collection also contains letters in Hebrew to Hamizrachi, from Joseph Seff, vice president of the Federation of American Zionists and rabbi of Congregation Anshe Alt Constantin in New York City, mentioning Turkish restrictions on the entry of Jews to Eretz Israel and urging the employment of professional Zionist agitators and the publication of Zionist propaganda booklets. He severely denounces certain American Zionist and Jewish leaders, including Zvi Hirsch Masliansky (Folder 77).
Collection catalogued by repository.
Research access not restricted. Photocopies provided.

SK 3/82

HEBREW COMMITTEE OF NATIONAL LIBERATION (HCNL)

(Revisionist group in America organized in 1944 and guided by Hillel Kook (Peter Bergson) as "trustees" of a "Hebrew nation"; engaged in rescue activities in Europe and efforts to form a Jewish Army and to establish a Hebrew national home in Eretz Israel.)
Ca. 30 linear feet, covering years 1944-1947, in Record Group HT 4.
In Jabotinsky Institute in Israel, Tel Aviv.

Collection consists of correspondence, minutes of meetings, newsclippings and reports documenting the following activities of members and supporters of the HCNL:

> aims and administration of HCNL; purchase of a building (Folders 1/1-3; 2/4); press conferences and public meetings (Folders 3/1 and 3/3);
> relations of HCNL with Zionist groups and organizations which were in conflict with the Revisionist movement, e.g., Zionist Organization of America and American Zionist Emergency Council; with groups and organizations within the Revisionist movement, e.g., New Zionist Organization, Political Action Committee for Palestine; with the Assirei Zion Fund, Inc. and the United Jewish Appeal of Greater New York (Folders 5/1, 3,5-9); and
> influencing governmental offices and institutions in America and abroad towards HCNL aims (Folders 6/2; 7/1,12,14; 9/1-4).

Among the institutions and offices figuring prominently in the collection are the Anglo-American Committee of Inquiry, the U.S. War Department and the U.S. War Refugee Board. These files also document the contacts of HCNL with several foreign embassies in America; activities of HCNL at the United Nations Conference on International Organization at San Francisco in 1945; and pressure by HCNL for free immigration of war survivors to Eretz Israel (Folders 1/9; 9/1-4).

Of special interest are the following:

> 23-page letter dated April 2, 1945 to Chaim Weizmann from Peter H. Bergson (Hillel Kook), urging Weizmann to join HCNL (Folder 1/6);
> 6-page declaration of principles and aims of HCNL, dated April 10, 1946, stressing the difference between "Jew" and "Hebrew", i.e., Jewish religion and Hebrew nation (Folder 1/6);
> 5-page memorandum by Eri Jabotinsky, dated March 22, 1944, suggesting that Jews be admitted immediately into Eretz Israel and that the postwar settlement include the establishment of a democratic and independent state (Folder 1/7);

letters dated June 20, 1946 to foreign ministers of 39 countries asking their support of the provisional government to be set up by HCNL (Folder 1/8);

letter dated July 15, 1946 from A. W. Cordier, assistant to the Secretary General of the United Nations, to Bergson thanking him for submitting the program for establishing a provisional government (Folder 1/8);

the 1946 plan of the HCNL for establishing the provisional government of the Hebrew nation in Eretz Israel (Folder 1/8); and

an extract dated April 28, 1944 from the United States Adjutant General's Office to the commanding general at Air Transport Control, instructing that the transportation of Eri Jabotinsky be aided by the United States Air Force to an unstated destination (Folder 7/11).

Collection catalogued by repository.
Research access not restricted. Photocopies provided.

SC 11/81

HEBREW UNIVERSITY, CONGRATULATORY SCROLLS
4 items, dated 1925, in Record Group 4° 1491.
In Jewish National and University Library, Jerusalem.

Items consist of inaugural ceremony greetings from four American universities: Yeshiva University, University of Tennessee, University of California, and Syracuse University, all bearing signatures of the respective presidents of the institutions. Professor Max Margolis is mentioned as representing the University of California (Folders 37; 70; 74; 76).

Of special interest is the lavishly illuminated scroll from Syracuse University, dated March 24, 1925, containing many biblical references and hailing the conversion of Mount Scopus from a scene of war to a seat of learning (File 76).

Collection catalogued by repository.
Research access not restricted. Photocopies provided.

SK 2/82

HECHT, BEN, 1894-1964
(American journalist, author and playwright; championed the

American League for a Free Palestine and the Hebrew Committee
of National Liberation.)
4 items, covering years 1947-1948, in Record Group PA 35.
In Jabotinsky Institute in Israel, Tel Aviv.

Collection consists of the following newsclippings: a letter by
Hecht to anti-British terrorists in Palestine supporting their aims
and methods and exhorting all Americans to do likewise and to
contribute to their cause; strong negative reaction by readers of the
New York Herald Tribune; and an advertisement for the American
League for a Free Palestine that includes a poem by Ben Hecht
entitled "Song of a Palestinian," expressing the anger and depres-
sion of the Hebrew soldiers because help is slow to arrive.
Collection catalogued by repository.
Research access not restricted. Photocopies provided.

TG 12/81

HERTZ, JOSEPH HERMAN, 1872-1946

(Born in Slovakia; moved to New York at age of 12; rabbi in Johan-
nesburg, South Africa, 1898-1913; early Zionist and co-founder of
the South African Zionist Federation; Chief Rabbi of the British
Empire 1913-1946.)
5 items, covering years 1898-1899, 1929-1930, interspersed and in
special folder in Record Group A 354.
In Central Zionist Archives, Jerusalem.

Collection includes the following pertinent items:

three handwritten letters dated 1898-1899 from Adele and
Bertha Szold to Hertz, mentioning their attendance with
Henrietta Szold at Zionist mass meetings in New York and
Philadelphia. Among the speakers were Stephen S. Wise and
Richard Gottheil (Folders 1; 5I and 5E); and

two copies (89pp.; 76pp. plus photographs) of "Memorandum
on the Western Wall," reviewing the role of the Wall in Jewish
history, written by Cyrus Adler on behalf of the Jewish Agency,
submitted in 1930 to the Special Commission of the League of
Nations (Folder 29).

Collection catalogued by repository.
Research access not restricted. Photocopies provided.

SH 5/81

HISTORY OF THE YISHUV

(Miscellaneous material relating to the history of Jewish settlement in Eretz Israel from the mid-19th century until 1943.)

Ca. 1300 items, covering years 1847-1948, interspersed in Record Group 4/Sections 1-3, which also include photocopies of materials relating to Eretz Israel found in the American Jewish Historical Society, Waltham, Mass.: Emily Solis-Cohen Papers, materials pertaining to the School of the Parents Education Association in Jerusalem and the Ehrenreich Papers (P-26)—all found in File 3/24 of the collection.

In Yad Yitzhak Ben Zvi, Jerusalem.

Collection includes correspondence, record books (*pinkasim*), pamphlets, reports and other documents relating to the following:

American immigration and tourism to Eretz Israel in the early decades of the 20th century; letters of recommendation (Folders 2/1; 3/3-5); questionnaires (Folders 3/3/1-29) and a *pinkas* (Folder 2/1/20) of Kollel America; labor immigration during 1930s and 1940s reported by the Histadrut (Folders 3/10,11); statistical data on immigration and tourism from the United States in annual reports of the Department of Migration (1936 in Folder 3/12; 1938 in Folder 3/17) and monthly bulletins of the Office of Statistics (February 1938 in Folder 3/21; May-June, 1938 in Folder 3/12; May, 1943 in Folder 3/21); and visits by Americans to Eretz Israel in the first decades of the century recorded in visitors books of the Talmud Torah of the Mea Shearim Yeshiva (Folders 2/1/23; 3/6/1) and Shaare Zedek Hospital (Folder 2/8).

Endorsement by American Consul Thomas R. Wallace, among others, of the aims of the Kehillat Jacob Society, established for agricultural interests in the Holy Land in 1909 (Folder 2/1/1).

Americans owning land in Jerusalem during the Ottoman period (Folder 2/1/5, in Turkish; Folders 2/1/2-4); and American Zion Commonwealth lands in Afula in 1925 (Folder 3/26/3).

Varied activities of Americans in Eretz Israel in the 1920s as described in Zionist Press Commission bulletins (Folders 3/15,16).

Social, cultural and scientific contributions of Americans residing in Eretz Israel, including Henrietta Szold and the Hadassah Medical Organization (Folder 3/18/1); Henrietta Szold and Nathan Straus in social services for the Jewish community (Folder 3/18/10); and Isaac B. Berkson in his summary and evaluation of the Department of Education for the 14th Zionist Congress.

Zionist activities in the United States in the late 19th century (Folders 2/6/28; 2/6/51; 3/24).

American funds sent to Eretz Israel during World War I via the Provisional Executive Committee (Folder 2/7/4).

American diplomatic activities relating to Palestine between 1897 and 1918 (in copies of files of the German Foreign Office in Bonn) (Folder 2/9).

Exchange of letters between Emir Faisal and Felix Frankfurter in March 1919, expressing willingness by Faisal to cooperate with the Zionists (Folder 3/19).

American Zionism in the 1920s as reflected in the bulletins of the Zionist Press Commission (Folder 3/15-16).

Hadassah Medical Organization 1922-1923 (Folder 3/18/1) as described to the United Nations Special Committee on Palestine (UNSCOP) in a memo submitted by the Vaad Leumi in 1947 (Folder 3/18/10).

Histadrut fundraising in 1920s-1940s (Folders 3/7,8,10).

Keren Hayesod fundraising 1931-1933 (Folder 3/22), 1939-1946 (Folder 3/25) in minutes and reports of these organizations.

Anglo-American Committee of Inquiry—public hearing and reports submitted to and by the Committee (Folders 3/13/28; 3/17; 3/22-23; 3/25).

Statements by American individuals and organizations criticizing British policy in Eretz Israel and/or supporting increased Jewish immigration and the establishment of a Jewish homeland: Felix Warburg, October 1930, upon resigning from his position at the Jewish Agency (Folder 3/27); James G. McDonald, 1944; Reinhold Niebuhr, 1942; American Jewish Committee, 1947 (Folder 3/22); Abba Hillel Silver, Moshe Shertok (Sharett) and David Ben Gurion in addresses at the United Nations, which Senator J. Howard McGrath of Rhode Island inserted in the Congressional Record, May 1947 (Folder 3/25); and the Jewish Agency to the Inter-Governmental Committee for Refugees, established by Franklin D. Roosevelt, 1939 (Folder 3/13/21).

Anti-Revisionist propaganda published by the Emergency Committee for Zionist Affairs in New York, 1940 (Folder 3/22).

"Zionism and the Arab World: Testimony," a pamphlet submitted to the Committee on Foreign Affairs of the House of Representatives, February, 1944 (Folder 3/6/8).

Fund raising in the United States for the Hebrew University Medical School in the 1930s (Folder 3/24, in the Solomon Solis-Cohen papers, photocopies from the American Jewish Historical Society, Record Group P-30).

Funds from America, some raised by Boris Schatz, for Bezalel School of Arts and Crafts during World War I and 1920s (Folders 2/7/4; 3/18/2).

Financial difficulties of Ephraim Deinard as a result of his publishing the weekly *Haleumi* in New York, 1888-1889 (150 subscribers), and formation of B'nai Zion Society for natives of Jerusalem in New York at that time (Folder 2/6/93).

Computerized index to 2/1-5 only.

Collection catalogued by repository.

Research access not restricted. Photocopies provided.

AF 2/82

IRGUN ZEVAI LEUMI, DIASPORA STAFF, PARIS

("National Military Organization"; armed underground organization founded in 1931; carried out armed reprisals against Arabs, and after British White Paper of 1939, against the British Mandatory authorities.)

1. Ca. 210 items, covering years 1926-1948, interspersed in Record Group K18.

In Jabotinsky Institute in Israel, Tel Aviv.

Collection includes correspondence, telegrams, financial statements and pictures pertaining to the dispatch of military and non-military supplies to the Irgun from America before the establishment of the State of Israel; relations among America-based organizations supporting the Irgun (American League for a Free Palestine and other Revisionist committees); disagreement among the Revisionists over acceptance of the United Nations partition plan; demands by Irgun supporters in America for a pro-Jewish foreign policy by the American Government in the Middle East conflict (Folders 2/8/1,4, 8-10; 2/18/12; 3/4,7; 5/1; 29/11).

Of special interest are the following:

1a. Orders in Hebrew and English (October 23, 1947) to recruit pilots for the Irgun in the United States and a list of names [of pilots?] including Americans: B. Litterman, P. Dubson, J. O'Neill, E. Macleod, E. Spector (Folder 4/1).

1b. Letter (May 5, 1948) from Abba Hillel Silver on behalf of the Jewish Agency to Dr. I. Lifschitz, executive director of the Palestine Emergency Fund in New York regarding an agreement between Haganah and Irgun that they establish a united front for national defense and that official Zionist institutions in Eretz Israel and abroad would not give the Irgun any allocations from campaigns conducted for defense purposes (Folder 6/5).
Collection catalogued by repository.
Research access not restricted. Photocopies provided.

DF and TG 2/82

2.   Ca. 24 items, covering years 1947-1948, in special folder "Underground Publications" in Record Group V.1113.
In Jewish National and University Library, Jerusalem.
Folder 19/1 of the collection includes newsclippings, advertisements, correspondence and leaflets regarding fundraising and propaganda efforts by American Jews on behalf of underground activities in Eretz Israel; and in favor of United States intervention to enforce the United Nations partition plan. Correspondents and signatories include Ben Hecht, Will Rogers, Jr., David Kay and Maurice Rosenblatt.
Of special interest are the following:
2a. Letter (July 23, 1947) from Hillel Kook (Peter Bergson) to President Harry S Truman requesting his assistance for the *Exodus 47* refugees and urging his direct intervention to break British resistance to Jewish immigration to Eretz Israel.
2b. A page from the United States *Congressional Record* (March 13, 1947) containing a speech by Congressman Hugh Scott of Pennsylvania, referring to the arrest of American crew members on the American-owned "illegal" immigrant ship *Ben Hecht* seized by the British authorities.
2c. Full-page advertisement from the *New York Post* (March 2, 1948) by the Palestine Resistance Defense Fund, denouncing the "embargo on the Hebrew People" by the State Department of the United States; reverse side contains an open letter from David Kay, president of Shell Products Company, Inc. condemning the "phoney diplomacy" at the United Nations and the rejection by Warren R. Austin in the name of the United States of direct enforcement of partition.

2d. Open letter, one of several, to the terrorists of Palestine by Ben Hecht published in the *New York Herald Tribune* (May 15, 1947), criticizing the American Jewish establishment for its lack of support for the Irgun and urging contributions to support underground movements in Eretz Israel.

2e. Memo (May 16, 1947) from Maurice Rosenblatt of the American League for a Free Palestine (ALFP) telling of friction between the various groups participating in the Palestine Resistance Committee and the withdrawal of the ALFP to form the non-political Palestine Resistance Fund as an exclusively financial channel to transmit funds to Jewish resistance movement in Palestine.
Collection catalogued by repository.
Research access not restricted. Photocopies provided.

SK 5/82

JABOTINSKY, ERI, 1910-1969
(Son of Zev Jabotinsky, active associate of Hillel Kook (Peter Bergson) in the United States during World War II.)
12 items, covering years 1940-1948, interspersed in Record Group A4.
In Jabotinsky Institute in Israel, Tel Aviv.

Collection includes correspondence and reports concerning: the establishment of the Jewish Aviation League of America and the Jabotinsky Aviation School which trained pilots for Zionist goals as well as for the United States Armed Forces; Stephen S. Wise favoring the establishment of a Jewish army; activities of the New Zionist Organization; activities of the Zionist Organization of America and the Committee for a Jewish Army (CFJA) in San Francisco; and involvement of American novelist and dramatist Meyer Levin in the production of a movie about Eretz Israel.

Correspondents include Stephen S. Wise, Dr. Klinger, Colonel Morris Mendelson, Isador (Israel) Goldstein, Irving Shore, Kurt Flaton and Yitzhak Ben Ami.

Of special interest is a carbon copy of a 5-page extract from a longer typed report, written after 1948, describing the activities of individuals and organizations involved in the formation, publicity and development of CFJA in America from 1939 to 1943. The author of the report, written in the first person, was someone closely associated with Hillel Kook and the CFJA leadership.

Collection not catalogued by repository.

Research access not restricted. Photocopies provided.

SA 1/82

JABOTINSKY, ZEV (VLADIMIR), 1880-1940

(Internationally prominent Zionist leader; soldier, author and poet; founder of the Zionist Revisionist Movement; played a leading role in the establishment of the Jewish Legion in World War I and served as a lieutenant in the unit.)

Ca. 125 items, covering years 1915-1940, interspersed in Record Group A1—private papers of Zev Jabotinsky.

In Jabotinsky Institute in Israel, Tel Aviv.

Collection includes both originals and photocopies of correspondence of Jabotinsky with Zionist leaders in America and Eretz Israel: Stephen S. Wise, Robert Szold, Julian Mack, Jacob De Haas, Abba Hillel Silver, Abraham Tulin, Chaim Weizmann and others (Volumes 4; 7; 8; 10; 34; 37), regarding support for armed Jewish forces during World Wars I and II and Revisionist activities in America. Among matters discussed are:

> affairs of the American branches of Betar (Revisionist youth movement) (Volumes 13; 35);
>
> activities of the New York Office of the Irgun Zevai Leumi (IZL) (Volume 25);
>
> American support and volunteers sought by Jabotinsky for a Jewish brigade in the British Army in World Wars I and II, both in direct appeals to American Congressmen and Senators and through his emissaries Benjamin Akzin and Robert Briscoe (Volumes 2; 25; 33);
>
> campaigning by Jabotinsky in 1922 for American pressure on Great Britain to implement the Mandate in accordance with the Balfour Declaration (Volume 4);
>
> American intervention sought by Jabotinsky against the British proposal to elect a legislative council in Palestine while the Jews were still a minority (Volumes 7; 37);
>
> request for American Jewish and governmental pressure and funds for the appeal of Abraham Stavski, accused of murdering Chaim Arlosoroff (Volumes 16; 35); and

developments in the American branches of the Zionists-Revisionists and contacts with other American Zionist groups in 1939-1940 as regularly reported by Jabotinsky from America to the presidium of the World Union of Zionists-Revisionists in Paris (Volumes 23-25; 36).

Of special interest are the following:

radiogram (May 12, 1934) from Jabotinsky to Stephen S. Wise including a cabled request to Louis D. Brandeis to pressure the American Government about the trial of Abraham Stavski and asking Wise to elicit support among his friends (Volume 6); and a 4-page letter (October 12, 1938) from Jabotinsky informing the Union of Zionists-Revisionists executive in London that he had met with United States Ambassador to Poland A. J. Drexel Biddle, who agreed to arrange a meeting between Revisionists and United States Ambassador to London Joseph P. Kennedy, for the purpose of obtaining an American veto of any change in the Mandate and toward convening an intergovernmental conference on the Jewish National Homeland (Volume 22).

There is also correspondence with Americans regarding the Hasefer Publishing Co., founded by Jabotinsky; requests directed to Stephen S. Wise and Abba Hillel Silver for aid in distributing a Hebrew Atlas and other publications of the company in America; and information concerning a translation into English and distribution in America arranged by Jabotinsky for his book *Samson* (Volume 28).
Collection catalogued by repository.
Research access not restricted. Photocopies provided.

MI and SA 4/82

JERUSALEM AND EAST MISSION/FUND (JEMF)
(Fund and Mission founded 1889 to support Anglican Church in Jerusalem and Middle East.)
1.   Ca. 650pp. of relevant items in 9 folders, covering years 1922-1946, in Jerusalem and East Mission Collection.
In St. Anthony's College Middle East Centre, Oxford.

Collection includes letters and reports of the Anglican Bishopric in Jerusalem dealing with the following subjects:

1a. Relations with the National Council, Episcopal Church of America (NCECA); correspondents include Rev. William Chauncey Emhardt, Executive Director of the Foreign Born Division of NCECA (Box XXIV, Files 4 and 5).

1b. Appointment and activities of an American representative on the staff of the Jerusalem Bishopric; correspondents include Bishop Rennie MacInnes (1870-1931), the Bishop in Jerusalem, 1914-1931; Reverend Edward M. Bickersteth, General Secretary, Jerusalem and East Mission, 1915-1935; Canon Charles T. Bridgeman, American Chaplain to the Bishop in Jerusalem, 1924-1929 and Canon of St. George's Cathedral, Jerusalem 1929-1944; and Frederick J. Bloodgood (Box XXIV, Files 4 and 5; Box XXV, Files 1 and 2).

1c. Relations between the YMCA and the Anglican Bishop in Jerusalem; disagreement in 1934 over allowing the official Nazi organ, *Völkischer Beobachter*, in the YMCA involving Bayard Dodge, former Secretary of YMCA in Jerusalem, and A. C. Harte, president of the American University of Beirut (Box XXV, File 3).

1d. Correspondence between Judah L. Magnes and the Anglican Bishop in Jerusalem regarding a compromise solution to the Royal (Peel) Commission Report proposed by Magnes in 1938: to limit immigration so that the Jewish population would not exceed 50 percent of the total population of Palestine, and later of Transjordan, in an independent state with autonomy for both Jews and Arabs (Box LXV, File 2).

1e. Evidence presented to the Anglo-American Committee of Inquiry on Palestine, 1946, prepared on behalf of the Bishopric by American Canon F. J. Bloodgood (Box LXVIII, File 1).

Of special interest is an undated (post-1924) "confidential memorandum concerning status of an American chaplain in Jerusalem," including an historical introduction and description of his functions mentioning the following subjects: American interest in Eastern churches as reflecting immigrant populations in the United States; generous support by American public as a function of direct American activity; American Protestants more interested in the work of Episcopal Church of America (ECA) than in the Church of England; political embarrassment in allowing aid to Palestine negated

by the dissociation of ECA from the Government of Palestine; and chaplain needed to serve the increasing number of American tourists and visitors (Box XXIV, File 5).
Handlist available in repository.
Research access not restricted. Photocopies provided for most items.

VL 6/82

2.   4 items, covering years 1900-1932, in Record Group MSS 2327-2340, among the papers of John Wordsworth, Bishop of Salisbury and President of JEMF, 1897-1911 and in General Correspondence of JEMF.
In Lambeth Palace Library, London.
Collection includes an undated letter from T. Batty to Bishop Wordsworth mentioning participation of the Bishop of California in an Easter Day service at St. George's Cathedral in Jerusalem ca. 1900 (MS 2327) and a letter (March 7, 1903) from Bishop Popham Blyth to Reverend Charles Richard Darcy Biggs discussing the American Presbyterian Mission and Archdeacon Frere (MS 2337/115).
Of special interest is a memorandum (May 1932) by Athelstan Riley on his work with Archbishop Edward Benson at the end of the 19th century, explaining differences between the Church of England and Americans over policy on relations with Eastern Churches; and noting the representation after 1924 by Canon Bridgeman of the Anglican Church of America on the staff of St. George's Cathedral in Jerusalem, where he especially kept in touch with Americans among the 1,200 Anglicans there. The reply (May 30, 1932) by E. M. Bickersteth is also relevant (MS 2331).
Published catalog of collection available: E.G.W. Bill, *Catalogue of MSS in Lambeth Palace* (Oxford, 1976).
Research access not restricted. Photocopies provided.

VL 6/82

JERUSALEM KOLLELOT
(Formally organized groups of Jewish immigrants in Jerusalem originating from the same geographic location in the Diaspora who subsisted on donations from their place of origin; their financial affairs and disputes with one another; includes Kollel America Tifereth Yerushalayim founded in 1896.)

1 item, dated 1912, in Record Group 4° 1203—Jerusalem Kollelot and Rabbi Meir Ba'al Haness Funds.
In Jewish National and University Library, Jerusalem.

Item consists of a *beth din* (religious court) verdict, dated 1 Adar 5672, involving Kollel America Tifereth Yerushalayim in Jerusalem's Mea Shearim Quarter (File 22).
Collection catalogued by repository.
Research access not restricted. Photocopies provided.

SK 3/82

JEWISH AGENCY, DEPARTMENT OF EDUCATION
5 items, dated 1919, in Record Group S2.
In Central Zionist Archives, Jerusalem.

Collection contains a letter mentioning the Federated Sons of Gallilea Palestine (in New York) as an organization dedicated to advancing the interests of settlers in the Galilee (Folder 6/I), and 4 letters from Henrietta Szold concerning the establishment of direct connections between the Department of Education of the Zionist Organization of America (ZOA) and the Education Committee of the Jewish Agency to aid the latter with American suggestions for experimental programs, methods, equipment and textbooks as well as to make Hebrew schools in America beneficiaries of educational development in Eretz Israel. Also mentioned are experiences of American educators who visited Eretz Israel and/or wished to teach there; the impending establishment by the ZOA of the Palestine Education Association to assist teachers desirous of preparing themselves for work in Eretz Israel; and a request from the Office of Education and Culture of the Jewish Agency, London to Washington Irving High School in New York City for its programs, regulations and reports (Folders 6/I and II).
Collection catalogued by repository.
Research access not restricted. Photocopies provided.

DF 11/81

JEWISH LEGIONNAIRES' ASSOCIATION OF AMERICA
(Membership composed of Americans who fought in the Jewish Legion in World War I; later called American Palestine Jewish Legionnaires, Inc.)
2 items, dated 1946, in Record Group K1.

In Jabotinsky Institute in Israel, Tel Aviv.

Items are newspaper ad and letter sent in 1946 by Elias Gilner (Ginsburg), national commander of the American Palestine Jewish Legionnaires to all members of the United States Congress, President Harry S Truman and the State Department urging all legionnaires to attend the meeting described in the advertisement and announcing a campaign to pressure Great Britain into fulfilling the Balfour Declaration and Mandate responsibilities (Folder 32).
Collection catalogued by repository.
Research access not restricted. Photocopies provided.

DF 12/81

JEWISH STATE PARTY, WORLD EXECUTIVE COMMITTEE, TEL AVIV

(Formed by dissidents of the Revisionist movement after their final split with Jabotinsky and followers in 1933; recognized the authority of the World Zionist Organization and participated in Zionist Congress elections; existed until 1946.)
12 items, covering years 1934-1937, in a special folder in Record Group L6.
In Jabotinsky Institute in Israel, Tel Aviv.

Folder 16 of the collection consists of correspondence with individuals in the United States, an information bulletin and Zionist Congress ballots pertaining to resolutions passed by the Jewish State Party at its first national conference, March 28-29, 1936 about Zionist activities in Eretz Israel and the United States; inner workings of the party and its efforts to attract a greater following; preparations for the 20th Zionist Congress and accusations of election violations; and a petition to the British Government against the partition plan of the Royal (Peel) Commission.
Collection catalogued by repository.
Research access not restricted. Photocopies provided.

DF 12/81

JOSEPH, DOV (BERNARD), 1899-1981

(Born in Canada; settled in Jerusalem in 1921 after serving in Jewish Legion during World War I; legal adviser, then member of Jewish Agency Executive; later military governor of Jerusalem, Minister of Supply and Rationing and Minister of Justice.)

Ca. 70 items, covering years 1920-1940s, interspersed in Record Group 5/4.

In Yad Yitzhak Ben Zvi, Jerusalem.

Collection includes correspondence, newsclippings and typed articles/reports regarding the following: activities of the Organization of American Jews in Palestine in 1923 (Folder 3); promotion of immigration and donations to Eretz Israel in 1921 by settlers from the United States (Folder 5); and proposal in 1939 by Irma Lindheim to the Palestine Council for Anglo-American Youth to establish a training farm in California to prepare American youth for pioneering (Folder 2/10).

Resident or visiting Americans mentioned in the correspondence include Judah Magnes, Alexander Dushkin, Louis Cantor, Louis Ehrlich, Mrs. Robert D. Kesselman and Tamar de Sola Pool (Folders 1-6) and there are articles and reports written by Judah L. Magnes, Gershon Agronsky (Agron) and Henrietta Szold (Folders 1-2).

The collection also includes correspondence, pamphlets and articles pertaining to political issues and Zionism. Among these are:

> ca. 20 personal letters written by Joseph to his wife Goldie between 1937-1947 commenting on the American Zionist scene; relations between American Zionists, especially Abba Hillel Silver and Israel Goldstein and World Zionist leaders; United States policy toward Palestine; Joseph's appearances before the National Conference for Palestine in 1937 and the Palestine Labor Conference at Carnegie Hall in 1944; his meetings with Felix Frankfurter, Louis Lipsky, Stephen S. Wise, Henry Montor; and the attitude of American Jews to partition (Folders 4/19-25,27,39; 5);
> articles on American Zionism in 1920, 1944 (Folders 2/11, 19); newsclipping from *The Palestine Weekly* of March 23, 1923 dealing with the conflict within the Zionist Organization of America two years previously between supporters and opponents of Louis D. Brandeis (Folder 6); and
> pamphlet prepared by American Zionist Emergency Council in January, 1948 surveying editorial opinion on United States policy toward Palestine (Folder 2/28).

Of special interest are the following:

a draft of a letter (10pp., incomplete, undated [1937?]) to David Ben Gurion from Joseph in New York dealing with efforts to promote support for partition among American Zionists; and with United States policy and the attitude of President Franklin Delano Roosevelt toward Palestine (Folder 4/27); and
a 32-page letter from Joseph to his wife (August 20, 1939) written at the 21st Zionist Congress in Geneva discussing the reaction of American Zionists and non-Zionists to the White Paper of 1939, particularly a speech by Solomon Goldman urging Zionists to follow a less belligerent course thereby provoking delegates from Eretz Israel (Folder 4/20).

There is also correspondence, reports and newsclippings reflecting contributions of Americans in the areas of education, social welfare and health services in Eretz Israel. Among these are:

American involvement in early years of the Hebrew University including a statement by Hebrew University officials to Montague D. Eder in 1925 that American donors support local rather than European executive control of the Hebrew University (Folder 1/3) and that Solomon Zeitlin was lecturing at the Institute of Jewish Studies in the summer of 1925 (Folder 1);
publications by Henrietta Szold in the field of social welfare (Folders 1-2) and a personal memoir of Henrietta Szold by Goldie Joseph (Folder 3);
Deborah Kallen's role in a summer camp at Athlit in 1934 (Folder 5); and
the program for the third commencement of the Hadassah Training School for Nurses, 1923 (Folder 5); and a *Palestine Post* supplement on health care published on the occasion of the opening of the Hadassah University Medical Center on Mount Scopus (May 9, 1939) with articles by Samuel Lewin-Epstein on dentistry and Bertha Landsman on infant care (Folder 1).

Collection catalogued by repository.

Research access not restricted. Photocopies provided.

AF 4/82

KAPLAN, ELIEZER, 1891-1952

(Born in Russia; settled in Eretz Israel in 1923; from 1933 to 1948, member of the Executive of the Jewish Agency in Jerusalem as head of its Financing and Administrative Department; first Minister of Finance of the State of Israel.)

14 folders and over 500 other items, covering years 1934-1947, in Record Group S53 among the papers of Eliezer Kaplan.

In Central Zionist Archives, Jerusalem.

Collection includes a folder devoted to settlement matters of Achooza "A", New York in 1938 (Folder 900); 4 folders dealing with immigration from the United States in 1936-1947 (Folders 578-581); see also *Guide to America and the Holy Land Studies*, I, p.59.

Also included are correspondence and reports concerning relations, particularly administrative and fiscal arrangements, between the Jewish Agency and various American Jewish organizations engaged in Zionist efforts, primarily activities of the United Palestine Appeal within the United Jewish Appeal:

> United Palestine Appeal (UPA): fundraising and financial reports; conventions; publicity; relations with the Zionist Organization of America (ZOA), Jewish National Fund and American Palestine Institute; opposing independent fundraising; *Jewish Morning Journal* special campaign for UPA in 1938 (Folders 241; 311-314; 322; 328-351; 365-366; 368-372; 391/I; 397; 402; 404; 425-426; 435/a-c; 441);
>
> Joint Distribution Committee (JDC) 1942-1947 (Folders 191/a-d; 192; 1614; 1616);
>
> United Jewish Appeal (UJA) 1937-1948: its goals, activities and constituent agencies—UPA, JDC and National Refugee Service; campaigns; budget; allotment committee; disagreements between JDC and UPA regarding allocation of funds; land purchase in Eretz Israel (Folders 329-330; 335-336; 340; 379; 386; 389-392; 398; 399/I);
>
> Keren Hayesod 1935-1948 (Folders 293/a-c; 315-318; 322-324; 365);

Office of the Jewish Agency in the United States 1943-1948
(Folders 241; 367); relationship of Zionists and non-Zionists
in Jewish Agency work (Folder 322);
American Jewish Conference in 1945 (Folder 1581); and
Council of Jewish Federations and Welfare Funds 1939-1947
(Folders 398-400).

Collection also includes correspondence and documents on the
following subjects:

Anglo-American Committee of Inquiry in 1946; material prepared for the committee and recommendations it made (Folders 1673; 2130);
influence of Jewish terror in Palestine on fundraising in the
United States during 1946-1947 (Folder 397);
revisionist activities in the United States during 1942 (Folder
500); and
various aspects of Zionist activity in the United States 1935-
1948 (Folders 468-472; 2031).

In addition to letters and reports exchanged by Henry Montor
and Kaplan, the collection includes correspondence between Kap-
lan and various Zionist and non-Zionist Jewish leaders including
David Ben Gurion, Jacob Blaustein, Louis D. Brandeis, Frank Cohen,
Felix Frankfurter, Israel Friedkin, Nahum Goldmann, Arthur
Hantke, Leo Hermann, Sidney Hollander, Louis Lipsky, Arthur
Lourie, Henry Morgenthau, Jr., Emanuel Neumann, Bernard
Rosenblatt, Charles Rosenbloom, Martin Rosenbluth, Abba Hillel
Silver, Julius Simon, Felix Warburg, Jonah B. Wise and Stephen
S. Wise.
Collection also contains material dealing with the following
aspects of United States-Eretz Israel economic ties:

employment of workers in Eretz Israel by U.S. companies in
1942 (Folder 1106);
payment and allocation of U.S. dollars by Jewish Agency; negotiations with Mandatory Government War Supply Board 1945-
1948 (Folders 1244-1248);
exhibitions in New York 1938-1947 (Folders 1253 a,b);

commercial ties with the United States 1938-1948: Palestine Economic Corporation 1943-1944 (Folders 1294-1296; 1951); Economic Enquiry Commission 1943, 1948 (Folders 1754; 1765); American Economic Council and details of various industries 1934-1937 (Folders 1914 a-f); United States shipping services 1939-1945, Gadinia-America Company 1937 (Folders 609 a,b); U.S. economic policy in the Middle East, especially regarding Eretz Israel and the oil factor 1945-1946 (Folders 2076; 2088); and
Elton Trading Corporation, New York 1945 (Folder 2177); Export-Import Bank/Bank of Washington policy statement 1945 (Folder 2184).

Also included is material on funds from the United States for Hebrew University 1934-1948 (Folders 1358 a-d) and its Department of Agriculture (Folder 1359); Hadassah Medical Organization, and Hadassah activities in the United States 1934, 1940-1947 (Folders 1382-1384); students from Eretz Israel in the United States in 1948 (Folders 2053).
Collection catalogued by repository.
Research access not restricted. Photocopies provided.

HK and TG 11/82

KEITH-ROACH, EDWARD, 1885-1954
(British colonial administrator in Palestine, 1919-1943.)
1 item, covering years 1919-1943, in the Keith-Roach Papers.
In St. Anthony's College Middle East Centre, Oxford.
    The item consists of two volumes of an unpublished auto-biography entitled "Pasha of Jerusalem," filled with references to activities of Americans in Palestine, such as the YMCA (pp. 34; 360; 584) and John D. Rockefeller (pp. 171, 363).
    Of special interest are references to the American Colony in Jerusalem (pp. 171, 326) and its dissolution: "after constant squabbles and charges and counter-charges of unfair treatment, it finally broke up and after protracted arbitration proceedings, the properties were divided among the different groups."
Collection uncatalogued.
Research access not restricted. Photocopies provided.

VL 6/82

KOOK, HILLEL (PETER BERGSON), 1915-
(Born in Lithuania; arrived in Eretz Israel 1925; leader in Revisionist affairs in the United States; established the Committee for a Jewish Army, Committee to Save the European Jews, Hebrew Committee of National Liberation, American League for a Free Palestine, 1941-1949.)
6 items, covering years 1944-1945, in Record Group PA 137.
In Jabotinsky Institute in Israel, Tel Aviv.

    Collection includes 6 handwritten quarto notebooks containing articles by Kook, Ben Hecht and others regarding the establishment of the Hebrew Committee for National Liberation; notes on the position of the Emergency Committee for the Rescue of Persecuted Jews of Europe regarding declarations issued by the White House, Fiorello La Guardia, Senators and the press in favor of establishing a federal agency to aid Jewish refugees in Europe and in their efforts to reach Eretz Israel; and drafts of a letter by Kook to Chaim Weizmann regarding the Jewish problem and suggestions for a solution.
Collection catalogued by repository.
Research access not restricted. Photocopies provided.

TG 12/81

KOPELOWICZ, AHARON
(Member of the New Zionist Organization (NZO) delegation to the United States during and after World War II.)
1 item, dated 1945, in Record Group PA 192.
In Jabotinsky Institute in Israel, Tel Aviv.

    Item is a telegram (November 8, 1945) from Samuel Friedman to Aharon Kopelowicz requesting his participation in the Washington demonstration on November 12, scheduled before the meeting between Prime Minister Clement Attlee and President Harry S Truman at which he believes the future of Palestine will be discussed.
Collection catalogued by repository.
Research access not restricted. Photocopies provided.

TG 12/81

LAMPERT AND GELMAN FAMILIES
(Among the Hovevei Zion settlers of Ekron in 1883.)
12 items, covering years ca. 1900-1929, in Record Group 5/3.

In Yad Yitzhak Ben Zvi, Jerusalem.

Collection includes Hebrew and Yiddish correspondence and a genealogical chart of the Gelman and Lampert families living in Eretz Israel and the United States; and a report of an interview with Beth Rosenbaum, describing the activities of her grandfather, Moshe David Gelman, in settling Ekron and in Zionist affairs in America.

Among the subjects discussed in the letters are the Arab riots in Jaffa in 1921 and assistance given to colonization in Eretz Israel by the American Zionist movement.

Collection catalogued by repository.

Research access not restricted. Photocopies provided.

SG 1/82

LEASSIRENU (PRISONERS' WELFARE SOCIETY)

(Society for attending to the needs of Jewish political prisoners/ detainees and their families from 1946-1948; negotiated with British authorities for transfer of Jewish prisoners from Arab areas and for repatriation of Jews deported to Kenya.)

1.   20 items, covering years 1945-1947, in Record Group HT 6.
In Jabotinsky Institute in Israel, Tel Aviv.

The collection includes correspondence from families of Jewish detainees requesting that the Anglo-American Committee of Inquiry investigate the condition of Jewish prisoners and visit the detention camps; a telegram from the committee of Jerusalem area prisoners asking New York lawyer Max Seligman to intercede with the High Commissioner to cancel his intended deportation of prisoners (Folder 2/5); reports of activities in the United States to aid families of Jewish detainees/deportees in Eritrea by David Bukspan, Eliezer Shostak and Seligman (Folder 3/15); and correspondence between Bukspan, Judah L. Magnes and the Joint Distribution Committee regarding its refusal to allocate money for families of detainees because it limits its efforts to aiding refugees in Europe (Folder 6/4).

Collection catalogued by repository.

Research access not restricted. Photocopies provided.

TG 11/81

2.   Ca. 43 items, covering years 1947-1948, interspersed in Record Group 40.
In Israel State Archives, Jerusalem.

Collection contains letters and telegrams to Moshe Shertok (Sharett) in New York from Leassirenu and relatives of Jewish prisoners held in Kenya requesting that everything possible be done to ensure the prisoners' release before termination of the Mandate (Folder 42), as well as correspondence requesting financial assistance from organizations in America. The latter also discusses the relations of Leassirenu with the Jewish Agency in New York and the American Fund for Palestinian Institutions (Folders 42 and 62).
Collection catalogued by repository. Description published.
Research access not restricted. Photocopies provided.

DF 2/82

LEVANON (BELLINKY) FAMILY
(Jerusalem family of Judge Mordecai Levanon who was born in Russia in 1888; served as president of the Yeshurun Organization in Jerusalem.)
3 items, dated 1943, in Record Group 5/12.
In Yad Yitzhak Ben Zvi, Jerusalem.
    Collection contains correspondence and curriculum vitae of Preiser, an American who settled in Eretz Israel in 1935 and later requested employment as a rabbi at Yeshurun Synagogue in order to qualify for a commission in the Chaplaincy Corps of the United States Army; one letter was sent to Alexander Lamport in the United States via Ethel Lamport of Tel Aviv (Folder 1).
Collection catalogued by repository.
Research access not restricted. Photocopies provided.

AF 4/82

LEVIN, MEYER, 1905-1980
(American novelist and dramatist; settled in Eretz Israel in 1958.)
2 items, dated 1947, in Record Group B—among the 16mm films.
In Israel Film Archives, Cinématheque, Jerusalem.
    Collection includes two feature-length films reflecting American involvement in film production in Eretz Israel:

> *The Illegals*: English, Hebrew, French and Spanish versions of the semi-documentary film about the *Berihah* movement across Europe and to Eretz Israel via ships; filmed in Eretz Israel; produced and directed by Meyer Levin; production company—Americans for Haganah (671B; 795B; 845B); and

My Father's House: story of a young boy searching for his parents and a young woman hoping to forget who meet as they land illegally in Eretz Israel; directed by Herbert Kline; photographed by Floyd Crosby; music by Henry Brandt; produced in Eretz Israel by Herbert Kline and Meyer Levin; screenplay by Meyer Levin based on his book (1131B).

Collection catalogued by institution.
Research access not restricted. For use in institution.

RA 5/82

LEVY, JOSEPH, 1899-1965
(Born in Jerusalem; studied journalism and languages at the American University in Beirut; Jerusalem correspondent for the *New York Times* 1928-1929; assignment expanded to the entire Middle East, 1930-1948.)
Ca. 235 items, covering years 1928-1951, in Record Group 72—in special folders.
In Israel State Archives, Jerusalem.

Collection contains personal and business letters, telegrams, background material, reports, newsclippings, drafts of agreements, drafts of articles concerning Levy's work as Middle East correspondent for the *New York Times* as well as other personal and professional activities during that time.

Material includes: comments on articles by Levy for the *New York Times* (Folders 695/1,2,3). Among the correspondents are Nathan Straus, Roger Straus, Rose Halperin, Emanuel Neumann and H. Pereira Mendes.

Reports by Lewis French in 1931 and 1932 about land settlement and development in Palestine, including memoranda submitted by the Executive of the Jewish Agency on the French reports and drafts of articles based on the reports (Folder 695/1).

Unofficial reports and letters from Jamor F. Goldsmith (Goldie) on the situation in Palestine from 1936-1940 (Folder 695/2).

Despatches and personal letters to Levy written by Yusif Hana (1935-1940) of the Jaffa-based Arabic newspaper *Falastin*, concerning the Arab position in the Arab-Jewish conflict as well as internal Arab affairs in the Middle East (Folder 695/5,6).

Reports on the pro-Nazi organization in Syria and Nazi activities in Lebanon (Folder 695/7).

Drafts of articles on Palestine submitted to the *New York Times* (Folder 695/10).

Relationship of Levy with Judah L. Magnes and their cooperation on a number of projects including activities of Ihud (association to promote Arab-Jewish understanding) in New York (Folders 695/3,4).

Of special interest in the collection are the following:

Confidential letter from High Commissioner Arthur Wauchope (May 15, 1936) to Levy expressing distress over reports that the American press describes the situation in Palestine as "such that there is no security either for person or property," and the hope that Levy will use his influence to prevent any "exaggerated" reports (Folder 695/2).

Ca. 26 documents (1928-1939) dealing with efforts by Judah L. Magnes and Levy with the cooperation of H. St. John Philby to achieve a joint Arab-Jewish agreement on Eretz Israel, including a draft agreement "as a solution of the existing political situation in Palestine," which received the consent of the Grand Mufti (Folder 695/4).

Letters and telegrams (May-July, 1944) concerning efforts to rescue Hungarian Jews by the War Refugee Board with the cooperation of the Turkish government and various Jewish organizations. Persons figuring prominently in the correspondence include Ira A. Hirschmann, the War Refugee Board delegate in Turkey; Laurence A. Steinhardt, United States Ambassador to Turkey; Judah Magnes and Henrietta Szold. Organizations represented at the various meetings include the American Joint Distribution Committee, the Jewish Agency, the Rescue Committee of Agudat Israel, the Histadrut, and HICEM (Folder 695/3).

A 5-page copy of a translated letter (November 29, 1938) to President Franklin Delano Roosevelt from Abdul Aziz el Faisal (Ibn Saud), king of Saudia Arabia, stating that there is too much American support for the Jews in Palestine and asking Roosevelt and the American people to accept his view that the Jews have no present nor historical claim to Palestine (Folder 695/6).

Exchange of telegrams (December 1936) between the *New York Times* office and Levy regarding the requested dismissal of Levy's assistant James Ginzburg for misquoting testimony presented by Chaim Weizmann at the Palestine Royal (Peel) Commission (Folder 695/2).

Collection catalogued by repository.
Research access not restricted. Photocopies provided.

HK 4/82

LOHAMEI HERUT ISRAEL (LEHI or STERN GROUP)
(Armed underground organization in Eretz Israel founded by Avraham Stern; broke away from the Irgun Zevai Leumi during World War II.)
6 items, covering years 1947-1948, in Record Group K 5.
In Jabotinsky Institute in Israel, Tel Aviv.

Collection includes an issue of the New York newspaper *Jerusalem Calling* criticizing British and American policy on the Jewish-Arab conflict (Folder 5/3); discussions with representatives of the Anglo-American Committee of Inquiry and a communication from Teheran to the Jewish Agency in Jerusalem, including a letter sent to the American embassy in Teheran purportedly by a Jewish group intending to kill British officials (Folder 5/1).
Collection catalogued by repository.
Research access not restricted. Photocopies provided.

DF 12/81

MALTA BIBLE SOCIETY
(Malta was the advance base for missionary work and Bible distribution activity in the Near East in the first half of the 19th century.)
Ca. 20 items, covering years 1820-1834, 1845, in the Minutes of the Malta Bible Society.
In British and Foreign Bible Society, Bible House, London.

Collection includes short summaries of letters from Pliny Fisk, Jonas King and other American missionaries. The Letter Book of the Rev. J. Lowndes, BFBS agent in Malta, contains a letter (July 24, 1845) to Edward Robinson's associate, Rev. Eli Smith, offering to furnish him with Bibles and letters to William Goodell.
Collection catalogued and indexed by repository.
Research access not restricted. Prior arrangement advised. Photocopies provided.

VL 1/82

MANDATORY GOVERNMENT, ADMINISTRATOR GENERAL
(Responsible for administrative procedures, involving the registration

of companies, partnerships, patents and designs, trademarks and the official receiver in bankruptcy.)
Ca. 15 items, covering years 1945-1947, in Record Group 29.
In Israel State Archives, Jerusalem.
　　Collection contains the following relevant material:

> letters, circulars, press releases and United Nations resolutions concerning procedures for working with the United Nations Special Committee on Palestine (UNSCOP), including names and functions of the 57 members of the UNSCOP Secretariat, 20 of whom were American (Folder OR/225);
> personal and confidential circulars regarding general administrative procedures to be followed in working with and supplying information to the 12-member Anglo-American Committee of Inquiry (Folders OR/203; ADMS/32); and
> a description of the newly created post of attaché for colonial affairs in Washington and procedures for supplying information to him (Folder OR/230).

Collection catalogued by repository.
Research access not restricted. Photocopies provided.

HH 2/82

MANDATORY GOVERNMENT, ATTORNEY GENERAL
Ca. 240 items, covering years 1922-1947, interspersed in Record Group 3.
In Israel State Archives, Jerusalem.
　　Collection includes documents regarding relations between the United States Government and the British Mandatory Government in the following areas:
　　The Anglo-American Committee of Inquiry: 7 documents of routine administrative nature, dated 1945-1946, including a description of land problems in Palestine (Folder 702).
　　The United States/Great Britain convention on laws pertaining to the disposal of real and personal property belonging to Americans in Palestine: 4 letters dated 1941 concerning wartime control of money leaving Palestine (Folder 706).
　　The status of Palestine and restrictions connected with the United States Neutrality Act of 1939: 4 letters from January-April, 1940 (Folder 724).

Seizures of American ships during the years 1939-1945 in the vicinity of Palestine by the British authorities, who suspected that the country of destination may have been trading with the enemy or that the cargo may have contained contraband goods: 7 folders, each containing ca. 15-45 summonses, bills of lading and correspondence regarding routine legal matters (Folders 738-739).

The United States/Great Britain convention on the Palestine mandate regarding American interests and the United States/France convention regarding the mandate for Syria and Lebanon: 20 items of varying length (1-13 pp.) dated 1922-1924, consisting of correspondence, proposals and drafts of treaties. Correspondents include Winston Churchill; Lancelot Oliphant; James Henry Thomas; Myron T. Herrick, U.S. Ambassador in Paris; Raymond Poincaré, French Foreign Minister; Ramsay MacDonald; and Frank B. Kellogg, United States Ambassador in London (Folder 756).

The collection also includes correspondence between the Attorney General and American Zionist leaders and minutes of meetings dealing with various legal matters regarding the establishment of the Hebrew University such as tax deductible contributions, import duty exemptions, awarding of loans, and legal status of the Hebrew University. Correspondents include Judah L. Magnes, Julian Mack, Attorney General Norman Bentwich, Harry Sacher, Robert Szold and Frederick H. Kisch (Folder 757).

Collection catalogued by repository.

Research access not restricted. Photocopies provided.

HK 9/81

MANDATORY GOVERNMENT, CHIEF SECRETARY'S OFFICE
Ca. 37 items, covering years 1918-1925, interspersed and in special folder in Record Group 2.
In Israel State Archives, Jerusalem.

Collection includes material pertaining to the following:

Fund raising for Keren Hayesod in various American cities and disagreement among American Zionists over control of Keren Hayesod funds raised in America (Folders 37; 145; 146).

American congressional support for a Jewish national homeland in Palestine in 1922 (Folder 145).

New York organizations connected with Eretz Israel in 1922: Palestine Cooperative Company Inc.; Palestine Foundation Fund;

and Zionist Organization of America, together with a list of its members (Folder 146).

Political activities of World Zionist leaders and their suggestions for the boundaries of Eretz Israel, mentioning such American leaders as Harry Friedenwald, Robert Szold, Julius Simon, Benjamin V. Cohen, Louis D. Brandeis and Bernard Flexner (Folders 36; 139; 142; 143; 145 and 146); in the minutes of the October 20, 1920 meeting of the Executive and Political Committees of the World Zionist Organization in London, Chaim Weizmann urged that American Zionists press for rejection by the American Government of French claims to the Yarmuk River which would endanger the Rutenberg hydro-electric project (Folder 139).

Emir Faisal's reactions to his first meeting with American Zionists: 5 copies of his letter to Felix Frankfurter dated March 1, 1919 (with a British Government cover note dated June 5, 1925), expressing Arab sympathy with the proposals submitted by the World Zionist Organization to the Paris Conference: ". . . there is room in Syria for us both . . . neither can be a real success without the other" (Folder 176).

Documents regarding the King-Crane Commission of the Paris Peace Conference dealing mainly with technical procedures and itinerary (Special Folder 239).

Of special interest are the following:

A 4-page memorandum by Chaim Weizmann, dated July 23, 1923, describing his March 3-19 visit for Keren Hayesod fundraising campaigns in various American cities, where he met with Louis Marshall, Irving Lehman, Herbert Lehman, Nathan Straus, Oscar Straus, Julius Rosenwald and Cyrus Adler. Noting an improvement in American Jewish sentiment toward reconstruction in Eretz Israel especially among influential and more Americanized Jews, Weizmann comments that the 3,300,000 American Jews "are at present the most powerful force in the Jewish World, and their moral and financial support . . . is a factor of almost incalculable importance" (Folder 146).

Copy of a joint resolution introduced in the United States Senate on April 10 and House of Representatives on April 19, 1922, declaring that the "United States of America favors the establishment in Palestine of the national home for the Jewish people in accordance with the . . . Balfour Declaration" enclosed with a diplomatic despatch from the British ambassador in Washington to the London Foreign Office (Folder 145).

A 2-page "secret" report from Chief Administrator Arthur Money to the Chief Political Officer, dated June 23, 1919 in which the former expresses dissatisfaction with the fact that the King-Crane commissioners were under the influence of William Yale, referred to as an agent of the Standard Oil Company who prevented them from meeting the pro-British American Colony in Jerusalem while arranging for them to meet with delegations voicing a strong predilection for an American mandate. British fears that pro-American feelings of the population might lead to an American mandate are also expressed in despatches dated May 2, 1919 (Folder 239 in its entirety).

Collection catalogued by repository. Published catalog available.
Research access not restricted. Photocopies provided.

TG 4/81

MANDATORY GOVERNMENT, DEPARTMENT OF AGRICULTURE AND FISHERIES

Ca. 5 items, covering years 1936, 1942-1948, interspersed in Record Group 7.

In Israel State Archives, Jerusalem.

Collection contains correspondence of an American agricultural expert, O. S. Morgan, professor of agricultural economics and representative of the Near East Foundation, who came to Palestine to survey agricultural conditions in 1942 (Folder Ag6).

Collection catalogued by repository.
Research access not restricted. Photocopies provided.

DF 3/82

MANDATORY GOVERNMENT, DEPARTMENT OF ANTIQUITIES, EXCAVATIONS

Ca. 925 items, covering years 1920-1948, interspersed in 26 folders of Record Group ATQ 169 (1920-1926); ATQ 6 (1926-1948).

In Archeological (Rockefeller) Museum, Jerusalem.

Collection includes correspondence and a variety of documents chronologically arranged regarding administrative details of archeological excavations in Palestine sponsored by American institutions and/or conducted by American archeologists in cooperation with the Department of Antiquities of the Mandatory Government at the following sites: Beisan (Bet Shean); Tell en Nasbeh; Kulat Kurein (Montfort); Megiddo; Bet Shemesh (Ayn Shams); Tel Bet Mirsim; Khirbet et Tubeikah; and Tell el Ful.

Sponsoring American institutions and their excavators corresponded with officials of the Department of Antiquities: John Garstang; Phillip L. O. Guy; Leo A. Mayer; and others; and directors and officials of other departments of the Mandatory Government: Lands; Customs; Immigration; Prisons and the various districts.

Administrative details common to all excavations include granting permits for soundings and excavations; exemptions from immigration duties on archeological and scientific equipment needed for excavation; importing and exporting antiquities discovered during excavations; travel facilities extended to excavators; leasing or expropriating land at excavation sites; health (malaria), security (theft and vandalism) and labor (imported versus local) issues; legal agreements between Department of Antiquities and sponsoring institutions concerning loan of antiquities; division of antiquities uncovered during excavations; and reports and descriptions of archeological sites and artifacts.

Of interest throughout the collection are descriptions by Americans traveling in Palestine; meetings and conferences with well-known political figures and scholars; references to political, economic, social and climatic conditions in Palestine; and personal correspondence reflecting the relationship of colleagues in pursuit of similar scholarly endeavors and the sharing of scientific knowledge and data by archeologists in America and Palestine, e.g., letter (December 21, 1928) from William Bade to the Department of Antiquities describing the treatment of artifacts to reveal decoration.

The collection contains information on the following sites:

Beisan—ca. 375 items interspersed in 9 folders of ATQ 169 and ATQ 2/6, covering years 1920-1946; sponsor: University Museum of Pennsylvania, Philadelphia, Pa.; excavators: Clarence S. Fisher, Alan Rowe, Gerald M. Fitzgerald.

Of special interest are the following:

a letter (September 9, 1922) to the director of antiquities from the chief inspector of antiquities, Phillip L. O. Guy, regarding a fire near the excavation site. Clarence S. Fisher, as field director, was held liable for resultant damages. The matter was referred to the American Consul in Jerusalem; and

a letter (October 25, 1928), in Hebrew with its English translation, to the Department of Antiquities from Boris Schatz, director of the Bezalel School of Arts and Crafts, concerning repair of a plaster model of the stelae sent to the Palestine Museum by the University Museum in Philadelphia. The official letterhead of the Bezalel School lists four Americans among its founders: J. Schonthal, Abba Hillel Silver, Joseph S. Bluestone and B. Shelvin.

Tel en Nasbeh—ca. 75 items interspersed in three folders of ATQ 169 and ATQ 3/6; covering years 1925-1948; sponsor: Pacific School of Religion, Berkley, California; excavator: William Bade. Americans figuring prominently in the correspondence besides Herman H. Swartz, president of the Pacific School of Religion, include the following members of the scientific staff on the expedition: Elihu Grant of Haverford College, Pennsylvania; W. C. Gotshall, engineer; Clarence S. Fisher; George P. Hedley.

Of special interest are the following:

a memo by William Bade (March 13, 1927) to the Department of Antiquities listing his proposed scientific staff for the excavation, handwritten on the reverse side of a printed advertisement for the Archeological Congress in Palestine and Syria in April, 1926; and

a letter (June 30, 1929) handwritten by Bade to Mr. Lambert at the Department of Antiquities reporting the discovery of an Iron Age Tomb at the site, with an enclosed note on other discoveries at the Tell and his conjecture that the site is the ancient city of Mizpeh.

Kulat Kurein (Montfort)—ca. 45 items interspersed in two folders of ATQ 169 and ATQ 4/6; covering years 1923-1931; sponsor: Metropolitan Museum of Art, New York City; excavators: Bashford Dean, W. L. Culver.

Megiddo—ca. 250 items interspersed in six folders in ATQ 169/ 1.2 and ATQ 7/6; covering years 1920-1947; sponsor: Oriental Institute of the University of Chicago, James H. Breasted, director;

excavators: Clarence S. Fisher, Phillip O. Guy, Gordon Loud, Ralph B. Parker.

Besides officials of the Oriental Institute with whom the afore-mentioned archeologists corresponded, Americans figuring promi-nently in the correspondence include staff members Mr. and Mrs. E. De Loach, and Mrs. William Ewart Staples, Laurence C. Woolman, Robert Scott Lamon, Herbert Gorden May, Arthur Carl Piepkorn (photographer); John D. Rockefeller, Jr.; Emmet Reid of Johns Hopkins University and E. T. Newell, president of the American Numismatic Society, NYC. American universities prominent in the material include Yale, Princeton, Chicago and Johns Hopkins.

Of special interest are the following:

> 20 documents, dated 1928-1946, concerning the long unre-solved issue of expropriating lands at the Megiddo site for purposes of archeological exploration (ATQ 7/6/Jacket 2); and a letter from Breasted to John Garstang (December 18, 1924) mentioning that John D. Rockefeller, Jr., had pledged $60,000 for the excavation if Breasted raised matching funds (ATQ 169/1.2).

Bet Shemesh—ca. 50 items interspersed in two folders in ATQ 14/6; covering years 1927-1939; sponsor: Haverford College, Pennsyl-vania; excavators: Elihu Grant, Clarence S. Fisher, Alan Rowe. Americans figuring prominently in the correspondence include I. J. Wood of Smith College and William F. Albright. American scien-tific personnel included Charles Sumwalt, Joseph Wampler, William Gad, Donald McCowan, E. F. Beaumont and Mrs. Elihu Grant. Institutions mentioned include the American Friends Mission in Ramallah (Quaker School where the Grants resided) and the Ameri-can Schools of Oriental Research (ASOR).

Tel Bet Mirsim—ca. 50 items interspersed in two folders in ATQ 20/6; covering years 1926-1936; sponsors: American Schools of Oriental Research and Xenia Theological Seminary of St. Louis, Missouri (later Pittsburgh-Xenia Seminary); excavator: William F. Albright. Other correspondents include M. G. Kyle, president of Xenia Theological Seminary, who resided at the American Colony; C. C. McCown; Nelson Glueck; Millar Burrows; A. Saarisalo; and Henry Delweiler. Cyrus H. Gordon was a member of the scientific staff. Universities mentioned also include Yale and Johns Hopkins.

Khirbet et-Tubeikah (Bet Zur)—ca. 15 documents in ATQ 45/6; covering years 1931-1932; sponsors: Presbyterian Theological Seminary and American Schools of Oriental Research; excavators: O. R. Sellers and William F. Albright (adviser). Figures prominent in the correspondence besides Sellers and Albright include Nelson Glueck and A. Saarisalo.

Tel el Ful—ca. 20 items in ATQ 169/8 and ATQ 63/6; covering years 1922-1938; sponsor: ASOR; excavator: William F. Albright. Nelson Glueck, Elias Gelat and Johns Hopkins University also figure prominently in the correspondence.

Collection catalogued by institution.

Research access not restricted. Photocopies provided.

RA 4/81

MANDATORY GOVERNMENT, DEPARTMENT OF EDUCATION
Ca. 400 items, covering years 1925, 1937-1948, interspersed in Record Group 8.
In Israel State Archives, Jerusalem.

Collection contains letters, telegrams, memos, minutes, circulars, applications, floor plans, booklets, reports concerning American involvement with various educational institutions in Eretz Israel:

> administrative and technical matters pertaining to the Louis Brandeis Vocational School (including the Hadassah Vocational Guidance Center—its programs, activities, and development), the Alice Seligsberg Trade School for Girls and the Julian Mack School, including the controversy over the continuation of employment of Mrs. Kittner at the Seligsberg School, the appointment of Shlomo Bardin as director of the Brandeis Vocational Center and Bardin's contributions to the school (Folders 1057/2959/1/PE; 1060/3200/61); and
> technical and administrative matters concerning the Amal Trade School, Jerusalem (founded with the assistance of the Amalgamated Clothing Workers of America) the kindergarten and elementary school at Kefar Syrkin, Kefar Szold and the kindergarten at Kefar Warburg (Folders 1059/3024/71; 1060/3177/78; 1061/3255/78; 1061/3258/61).

Files also include: mention of Hadassah Organization's medical treatment of children from Etz Hayim Talmud Torah and Yeshiva

(Folder 1045/1757/52); copies of correspondence from Agudat Israel to Menahem Porush in America (Folder 1042/1626/51); educational visits to the United States by teachers of the Hebrew Teachers College for Women and Herzlia Hebrew Gymnasia (Folders 1028/1175/66; 1028/1179/66); mention of two Hebrew Gymnasia students who enlisted in the United States Army and were killed in World War II (Folder 1026/1134/58); Deborah Kallen as headmistress of Julian W. Mack School in Jerusalem (Folder 1056/2859/36/PE); and addresses given by Herbert Lehman and Judah L. Magnes (Folder 1031/1236/61).

Correspondents include Judah L. Magnes, Shlomo Bardin, Julia Dushkin and Joseph Bentwich.
Collection catalogued by repository.
Research access not restricted. Photocopies provided.

HK/DP 3/82

MANDATORY GOVERNMENT, DEPARTMENT OF HEALTH
Ca. 338 items, covering years 1925-1947, interspersed in Record Group 10.
In Israel State Archives, Jerusalem.

Collection contains correspondence and documents regarding notification and registration of deaths of American subjects (tourists and residents) in Palestine and technical procedures for shipping the deceased to and from Eretz Israel and the United States for interment. Correspondence is primarily between the American Consulate and the Department of Health (Folders 5732; 5734-41/1645N; 2512/1574N).

The collection also includes correspondence, lists, blueprints, brochures, reports and minutes of meetings concerning American involvement in the establishment, maintenance and administration of various hospitals and health facilities in Eretz Israel:

Hadassah Voluntary Hospitals in Safed and Tiberias—the latter was reopened as the Albert Schweitzer Hospital for convalescence and hot baths in 1932; directed by Dr. Abraham Cohen from the United States; Henrietta Szold is among the correspondents (Folder 2149/1561N).

Hadassah Hospital, Mt. Scopus—construction in 1936-1937 administered by Julius Golub and supervised by Julius Lasker,

Americans who were brought to Eretz Israel for this purpose (Folder 2176/1561/N).

Nathan and Lina Straus Health Center in Jerusalem—public relations activities in 1932-1937 directed by American educated and trained Dr. Abraham J. Levy; lectures given by United States Consul George Wadsworth and United States public health official Dr. C. Turner (Folders 2372; 2373/1567N).

Central Kupat Holim Hospital in Afula—the establishment of an x-ray clinic by Dr. N. Rothenoff, president of the Federation of American Physicians; financial contributions by Hadassah women and American physicians toward construction of the hospital in 1929 (Folder 2158/1561N).

Marquis Medical Center in Jerusalem—requests by Miss Quincy Smith for permission to raise funds and construct building in 1937 (Folder 2195/1562N).

The collection also contains health literature and reports, dated 1926, on chlorination and water supply and purification from the United States Department of Health Services, Washington (Folder 380/1513N), and correspondence regarding all aspects of the visit by Dr. J. Allen Scott to Palestine on behalf of the International Health Board of the Rockefeller Foundation because of the incidence of hookworm disease in the Jaffa district during 1932 and 1937 (Folder 988/1535N).

Collection catalogued by repository.

Research access not restricted. Photocopies provided.

DR 11/81

MANDATORY GOVERNMENT, DEPARTMENT OF MIGRATION
Ca. 2600 items, covering years 1920-1935, interspersed and in special folders in Record Group 11.
In Israel State Archives, Jerusalem.

Collection contains letters, memos, telegrams, press clippings, statistical and other reports dealing with all aspects of travel and immigration to Palestine by citizens or individuals arriving on American ships, mostly for short visits:

categories of visitors: American tourists on cruises or United States warships (Folders 1151/30; 1236/2,25; 1237/4; 1238/36;

1239/1,2); American businessmen, clergymen, students, teachers, and participants in 1932 Maccabiah Games (Folders 1214/19; 1223/20; 1236/31,37,47; 1237/5; 1238/6,30,32,34,35); distinguished Americans who received special treatment and facilities, including Colonel Theodore Roosevelt, son of President Theodore Roosevelt as well as Jewish leaders Felix Warburg, Arthur Lehman and Cyrus Adler (Folders 1238/34-37);

statistics of Americans arriving in Palestine requested by the American Consul (Folder 1228/3); by the *American Jewish Yearbook* and Mount Carmel Bible School (Folder 1170/6); by the League of Nations (Folder 1227/66) and by Palestine Zionist Executive (Folders 1228/1,2); and

remittances to the Jewish Agency for costs of immigration certificates for immigrants arriving on American boats (Folders 1160/14,15) and the possibility of transferring these fees from the United States to Palestine (Folder 1160/12) are also discussed.

Collection also includes immigration certificate requests for Americans (Folders 1171/20 and 1179/12); matters pertaining to immigration of persons owning American Zion Commonwealth land (Folder 1181/29).

Of special interest are the following:

a 3-page handwritten memo (signature illegible), dated September 22, 1932, by an immigration officer noting the arrival at Haifa Port of *S.S. Vulcania*, whose 475 passengers, chiefly American tourists, included 175 immigrants of which 120 were from the United States (Folders 1151/6); and

a 2-page secret report dated June 5, 1920 from Captain E. I. Quigley to Major Courtney of the Central Intelligence Department Occupied Enemy Territory Administration in Jerusalem concerning the background and activities of Poalei Zion and Ahdut Haavodah in Eretz Israel. Mentioned as spreading socialist propaganda in the report are two "comrades" from America —"Fineman and Sirkin"—along with Yitzhak Ben Zvi, David Ben Gurion, and Berl Katznelson: ". . . up to the advent of the arrival of the American contingents the influence of the party was infinitesimal" (Folder 1155/10).

A major part of the collection contains letters, memos, lists, telegrams, correspondence, administrative documents and press extracts, dealing with all aspects of travel and immigration to Palestine by United States citizens or residents (Arab and Jewish) processed through the approximately 13 local branches of the British Consul in the United States (Folders 1142/1-5,15-18,26,27; 1143/3,4,7,8,13-15,22,23,28-34; 1144/4,6,10; 1150/9; 1151/6; 1170/6; 1171/20; 1172/18; 1179/12; 1181/29; 1185/47-49; 1187/14,24; 1201/33, 1207/1,2; 1214/19; 1220/49; 1236/2,25,31,32,37, 47; 1237/5; 1238/6,14,30,32,34-37), especially visa applications during the years 1924-1934 by Americans, mostly Jews, who upon arrival requested change to immigrant status; the stringent measures taken by the British and the strong response these measures elicited from the Zionist Organization of America (Folders 1142/16,17).

Mimeographed press reports issued by the Palestine Zionist Executive, the Jewish National Fund (Keren Kayemet) and Keren Hayesod, including summaries of funds raised in the United States (Folder 1223/20).

Other miscellaneous subjects dealt with in the material are the names of United States consular officials in Palestine 1928-1934 (Folder 1141/1); technicalities relating to British-American control of American travelers or those arriving on American warships (Folder 1150/4); litigation involving Americans or American companies (Folders 1152/20,23); issuance of emergency travel documents (Folders 1160/12,14,15; 1176/20,21); visas to United States for residents of Palestine, including American laws, regulations and quotas (Folders 1201/32,33; 1207/32; 1215/37); and helpful instructions for American Jews desiring to immigrate to Palestine appearing in an extract from *New Palestine* May 1, 1925 (Folder 1224/2).

Of special interest are the following:

Two letters of correspondence between Chief Immigration Officer Albert Hyamson and the British Passport Control Officer (B.P.C.O.) in New York, dated January 8 and February 10, 1931 respectively, Hyamson reports that "a certain number of United States citizens of Arabian nationality obtain visas as travellers and settle in Palestine . . . although in most cases no objection to the settlement of these people in Palestine is taken" (Folder 1142/16).

Five letters of correspondence during May and June, 1924 regarding the emigration of "rabbis" from Palestine to the United

States under the latter's policy of open immigration for clergymen (3/4 of all applicants for United States visas during a three month period). Hyamson fears the loss of credibility in the United States by the Palestine Government, commenting that every Jew who applies describes himself as a rabbi, when in fact it is "very exceptional for a genuine rabbi to emigrate to the United States," where rabbis visit presumably to collect charitable contributions (Folder 1201/33).

Correspondence dealing with the surplus of requests by rabbis (usually from Poland and Russia) to immigrate to Palestine and for laissez-passers of rabbis from Palestine to the United States, including a statement by Hyamson that "unpleasant attention to the scandal was being given in American circles" (Folder 1172/18).

Correspondence during the years 1922-1927 concerning visa applications of Arabs born in Palestine but residing in America. Included are instances of Arabs whose applications to British Consulate offices in the United States for visas to Palestine are referred to local Zionist bodies and complaints by Arab societies in New York about unfair treatment and difficulty in obtaining visas (Folder 1207/1).

The collection also includes letters, memos, telegrams, press reports and visa applications concerning technical procedures for visits by various scientific or cultural groups/individuals from the United States: experts on poultry, agriculture and health (Folder 1223/20); a team for water analysis from the American University of Beirut (Folder 1150/9); a one-month visit of American Variety Troupe entertainers (Folder 1214/19); a geological expert from Rockefeller Foundation (Folder 1238/35) and the visit of the Archeological Congress (Folder 1238/34).

There is also correspondence concerning the granting of visas to laborers (usually Egyptian) and scientific staff (usually American) for several archeological expeditions, under the auspices of the University of Chicago, the University of Pennsylvania, and the American Schools of Oriental Research (Folders 1150/9; 1185/47-49; 1187/14,24).

Collection catalogued by repository.

Research access not restricted. Photocopies available.

HK 1/82

MANDATORY GOVERNMENT, DIRECTOR OF CUSTOMS AND EXCISE (DCE)
Ca. 25 items, covering years 1927, 1932, 1947, in Record Group 128.
In Israel State Archives, Jerusalem.

Collection contains letters and circulars concerning: a proposal by the *New York Herald*'s advertising representative to the Director of Customs and Excise to attract American tourists to Palestine (Folder 554/26); and payment of duty on agricultural machinery brought in by two Americans who joined kibbutzim (Folders 1705/47; 1706/47).
Collection catalogued by repository.
Research access not restricted. Photocopies provided.

DF 5/82

MANDATORY GOVERNMENT, DISTRICT COMMISSIONER'S OFFICE, JERUSALEM
Ca. 54 items, covering years 1924-1946, in Record Group 23.
In Israel State Archives, Jerusalem.

Collection contains letters concerning the following subjects:

land dispute between Agudat Achim Anshei Amerika, which wanted to build a fence around its cemetery, and Arab villagers who claimed right of passage through it (Folder 854/28);
requests by American ministers of Christian denominations to the District Commissioner for the right to officiate at marriages (Folder 857/28); and
request by the District Commissioner's Office for confirmation that the American Friends Mission, Ramallah is complying with the law on the registration of marriages and divorces (Folder 857/34).

Collection catalogued by repository.
Research access not restricted. Photocopies provided.

DF 5/82

MANDATORY GOVERNMENT, DISTRICT COMMISSIONER'S OFFICE, LYDDA
Ca. 60 items, covering years 1945-1947, in Record Group 24.
In Israel State Archives, Jerusalem.

Collection contains letters, reports, circulars and minutes concerning the hearings before the Anglo-American Committee of Inquiry including presentations by Chaim Weizmann and David Ben Gurion on the position of American Jewry vis-à-vis Zionism and American Jewish political loyalty to the United States (Box 1841/ Files TA11806/A,B,C: TA11836).

Also included are legal notices for the expropriation of land for the United States Military Cemetery at Tel Litwinsky (Box 1791/ Folder S/4046).

Collection catalogued by repository.

Research access not restricted. Photocopies provided.

DF 2/82

MANDATORY GOVERNMENT, PUBLIC WORKS DEPARTMENT
Ca. 4 items, dated 1947, interspersed in Record Group 12.
In Israel State Archives, Jerusalem.

Collection contains 4 items of correspondence concerning a request by the American Consulate for the construction of security fencing (Box 97 Folder 4/26).

Collection catalogued by repository.

Research access not restricted. Photocopies provided.

DF 1/82

MANDATORY GOVERNMENT, RAILWAYS AND PORTS ADMINISTRATION
Ca. 40 items, covering years 1935-1939, interspersed in Record Group 28.
In Israel State Archives, Jerusalem.

Collection contains a 1935 letter to the Haifa port officer announcing the appointment of a Haifa agent for United States Lines (Folder 401); and letters, memos, lists, and certificates of registry concerning arrangements between the American and British Governments regarding permissible tonnage of American passenger ships for use in Palestine (Folder 406).

There is also a letter granting permission to the *New York Times* and United Press Association correspondents to enter the port area during the arrival of the Emperor of Abyssinia (Folder 471).

Collection catalogued by repository.

Research access not restricted. Photocopies provided.

HK 3/82

MANDATORY GOVERNMENT, REGISTRAR OF COOPERATIVE
SOCIETIES
(Registered and audited the books of Jewish and Arab cooperative
societies.)
Ca. 623 items, covering years 1919-1948, in Record Group 21.
In Israel State Archives, Jerusalem.

Collection contains letters, memos, constitutions, and certificates of incorporation relating to the registration of the following
societies and/or statements about their activities:

Young Men's and Young Women's Hebrew Association (Folder
3939/611); American Jewish Free Loan Fund (Folder 3939/253);
American Jewish Joint Distribution Committee (Folder 3939/119);
Constructive Aid Fund (*Keren Leezra Constructivit*) of Mizrachi
Women of America (Folder 3939/2185); American Daughters of
Rachel Aid Society (Folder 3939/622); Anglo-American Jewish
Association (Folder 3939/1176); American Jewish Physicians' Com-
mittee (Folder 3939/270); Kollel Chicago-Jerusalem (Folder 3939/
94); B'nai B'rith Youth (Folder 3939/2/2); United Synagogue of
America (Folder 3939/438); World Union of Zeirei Hehalutz and
Hapoel Hamizrachi and its branch in the United States (Folder
3939/737); Congregation Maramaros from America to Palestine
(Folder 3939/823); Hadassah Women's Zionist Organization of
America (Folder 3939/475); Nathan Straus Relief Station (Folder
3939/14); Anglo-American Society (for Americans of British
ancestry) (Folder 3939/102); Association of Foreign Correspondents in Palestine (Folder 3939/296); Palestine Medical Association
of the Alumni of the American University of Beirut (Folder 3939/
1097); American Christian Society (Folder 3939/191); American
Friends of Foreign Missions (Folder 3939/150); Independent Board
for Presbyterian Foreign Missions (Folder 3939/2098); American
Board of Missions to the Jews (Folder 3939/1883); International
Christian Scientist Association (Folder 3939/588); Near East Mission
of the Southern Baptist Convention (Folder 3939/244); American
Colony Aid Association in Jerusalem (Folder 3939/529); American
Schools of Oriental Research (Folder 3939/155); and the Young
Men's Christian Association and Young Women's Christian Associa-
tion with occasional reference to financial contributions from
America (Folder 3939/145 and 185).
Collection catalogued by repository.

Research access not restricted. Photocopies provided.

DF 6/82

MAPAI (LABOR PARTY), CENTRAL COMMITTEE

(Zionist labor party founded in 1930 by the union of Ahdut Haavodah and Hapoel Hatzair; founders included Berl Katznelson, David Ben Gurion, Yitzhak Ben Zvi and Joseph Sprinzak.)

10 items, covering years 1934-1947, interspersed in annual folders in Record Group 2.

In Labor Party Archives, Bet Berl, Tsofit.

Collection includes protocols, reports and other documents in Hebrew concerning trips by Mapai representatives to the United States for fundraising; immigration to Eretz Israel from America; attitude of American Jewry toward Eretz Israel; and increasing support for Mapai in America.

Individuals figuring prominently in the files include Golda Myerson (Meir), Felix Frankfurter, Louis D. Brandeis, Beba Idelson, David Ben Gurion, Stephen S. Wise, David Remez, Dov Joseph, and Eliezer Kaplan; organizations discussed include Hadassah, Haganah, the United Palestine Appeal, and the Joint Distribution Committee.

Of special interest is an 11-page report (February 19, 1947) by David Ben Gurion on his mission to America, including descriptions of Zionist Mapai support there.

Collection catalogued by repository.

Research access by consent of archivist. Photocopies provided.

SA 5/82

MAPAI (LABOR PARTY) OFFICE

5 items, dated 1945, in special folder in Record Group 2/25.

In Labor Party Archives, Bet Berl, Tsofit.

Folder 45 contains protocols in Hebrew dealing with a trip to the United States by Dov Pines to collect funds for Bet Berl and distribute books by Berl Katznelson; Mapai emissaries sent to the United States for the United Palestine Appeal; Habonim activities in America; and a report by Eliezer Kaplan on contacts with Abba Hillel Silver and the Joint Distribution Committee during his trip to the United States.

Collection catalogued by repository.

Research access by consent of archivist. Photocopies provided.

SA 5/82

MAPAI (LABOR PARTY) SECRETARIAT, MOVEMENT ABROAD

Ca. 360 items, covering years 1930-1948, in annual folders dealing with the United States in Record Group 2/101.

In Israel Labor Party Archives, Bet Berl, Tsofit.

Collection includes letters and publications, many in Hebrew, concerning developments in the Hechalutz Organization of America from 1934 to 1948 and correspondence between the American movement and its members who had already settled in Eretz Israel, mainly at Kibbutz Kefar Blum.

Ideological and financial problems of the American Hechalutz movement are dealt with by its emissaries Eliezer (Lazya) Galili, Joseph Israeli, Yona Goldberg and others; as well as the financial, cultural and agricultural activities of the three main training farms in the United States at Hightstown and Cream Ridge, New Jersey, and Allentown, Pennsylvania, as well as those of the kibbutz group in Baltimore, Maryland and the proposed farm in San Diego, California (Folders 34;46;47). Also discussed is the arrival in 1941 of the first group of Habonim members to form a kibbutz, which was first situated in Binyamina as the Anglo-Baltic kibbutz (Folder 41) and in 1944 moved to the Leon Blum colony at Naame (later renamed Kefar Blum) in the Huleh Valley (Folders 41-42;44-45).

Other matters discussed are distribution of *aliyah* certificates in the United States (Folder 34) and reports by emissaries of disagreements with other Zionist organizations such as Mizrachi and Hadassah, and especially with non-Zionist Jewish groups (Folder 34).

There are also letters of introduction to the central committee in Eretz Israel for American members of affiliated parties (Poalei Zion, Zeirei Zion) and requests for party assistance in their absorption (Folders 34;36-37).

Of special interest are reports concerning aviation courses arranged by Hechalutz for groups of prospective immigrants (*plugot aliyah*) planning to join the future Jewish army in Eretz Israel. Two groups of 20 men each finished the courses in 1944 and 1945 and awaited their *aliyah* certificates at training farms (Folders 41;44-45).

A major part of the collection includes correspondence, newsletters and leaflets regarding activities in America of Mapai, Poalei Zion, Zeirei Zion, Histadrut, Pioneer Women, the Jewish Agency, the Jewish National Fund, the United Jewish Appeal and the Zionist Organization of America as reported by emissaries of Mapai, who during the years 1930-1948 included many future Israeli leaders: David Ben Gurion, Levi Skolnik (Eshkol), Joseph Sprinzak, Zalman Rubashov (Shazar) and Shemuel Dayan, as well as other noted labor Zionists: Israel Mereminsky (Merom), Nachman Syrkin, Enzo Sereni, Eliyahu Golomb, Dov Hos, Eliezer (Lazya) Galili and Joseph Baratz. Their official duties included fund raising, organizing youth groups, correspondence with American administrations on Zionist ideas, and organizational assistance to Poalei Zion-Zeirei Zion, Pioneer Women, Jewish Labor League, and Hadassah. Also included are personal impressions of the state of American Zionism and American Jewish life in general (Folders 30-47).

Emissaries in 1930-1935 had difficulty filling their fundraising quotas due to the serious economic situation in the United States. Despite the surprisingly large sums raised for Eretz Israel during the Depression (Folders 30-33), the amounts were insufficient for the growing needs of the *yishuv*. Emissaries complained repeatedly about the American method of fund raising via lavish banquets and balls, which they felt both contradicted the pioneering spirit that the emissaries wished to convey to American Jews and wasted money that could have been donated to the *yishuv* (Folder 31).

During World War II, the emissaries dealt mainly with fund raising for refugee assistance, obtaining American visas for party members in Europe and directing American public opinion to the plight of European Jewry and against the British blocking immigration to Eretz Israel (Folders 40-46).

After the war, emissaries continued to seek aid for refugees in Europe but dealt mainly in fundraising for Haganah defense activities and Haganah ships bringing refugees to Eretz Israel (Folders 45-48).

Emissaries reported various meetings with American Zionist leaders such as Louis D. Brandeis, Nahum Goldmann, Stephen S. Wise, Robert Szold, Abba Hillel Silver, Hayim Greenberg and others (Folders 30-48).

There are many descriptions of American Jewish reactions to various events in Eretz Israel, such as the Arab riots in 1936 (Folder 36); the British blockade during the 1940s (Folders 41-47); the Peel Commission (Folder 37); the Anglo-American Committee of Inquiry (Folder 47) and the split in Mapai over the question of partition and matters of internal organization (Folder 44).

Also included are many Poalei Zion-Zeirei Zion circulars to members and the weekly publication *Yiddisher Kemfer* as well as numerous letters from American Jewish labor party officials to the central committee in Eretz Israel—all in Yiddish. American party secretary David Wertheim kept the party in Eretz Israel well informed of all internal debates and decisions in the united Poalei Zion-Zeirei Zion party (Folders 30-44).

Of special interest are the following:

travel journals from Ben Gurion's trip to the United States in May-June, 1935 in which he describes his fund raising tours and meetings with various influential American Jews, including Morris Rothenberg, Felix Warburg and Louis D. Brandeis (Folder 35);

telegram from David Wertheim, party secretary of Poalei Zion-Zeirei Zion to Cordell Hull, United States Secretary of State, dated March 25, 1938, citing the party's appreciation of the call issued by the State Department to governments to facilitate immigration to Palestine of victims of discrimination in Germany and Austria (Folder 38);

report of a meeting in March, 1937 between emissary Eliezer Kaplan and Louis D. Brandeis discussing the proposed partition of Eretz Israel (Folder 37);

an 11-page report by Ben Gurion to Eliezer Kaplan, dated September 14, 1937, when he met with Brandeis to discuss partition and the results of the Arab revolt, and with Benzion Apelboim (Ilan) and Israel Rosoff on training a Jewish army in the United States (Folder 37);

a letter, dated December 21, 1942, from emissary Arie Tartakower, reporting a meeting with Soviet representatives in the United States Constantine Oumansky and Maxim Litvinov to discuss the plight of Soviet Jewry, Polish refugees in the USSR and Zionist activists in Soviet prisons (Folder 42/vol. 1); and

minutes of a question and answer session Ben Gurion held in 1941 with members of Poalei Zion-Zeirei Zion at which Ben Gurion responded to questions about organizing a Jewish army, Jewish-Arab relations in Eretz Israel, relations between the Jewish Agency and the Mandatory Government and formation of a Jewish government before the formal establishment of a Jewish state (Folder 41).

The collection also includes correspondence between Mapai emissaries to the United States and its central committee in Eretz Israel regarding the following matters:

> requests by the New York Public Library and the American Federation of Labor for publications from Eretz Israel (Folder 47); founding of a Workers' College in Eretz Israel; party decision to continue this dream of Berl Katznelson after his death in 1944; repeated requests for funds and equipment (Folders 44; 48); and
> repeated requests by emissaries and by Poalei Zion-Zeirei Zion of America members for Zionist Socialist propaganda material for distribution among American Jewish youth to counteract the rising influence of Revisionist propaganda (Folder 47).

Collection catalogued chronologically by repository.
Research access by consent of archivist. Photocopies provided.

MI 3/82

MAPAI (LABOR PARTY) SECRETARIAT, PROTOCOLS

12 items, covering years 1931-1941, interspersed in annual folders in Record Group 2.
In Labor Party Archives, Bet Berl, Tsofit.

Collection includes protocols, lists and reports in Hebrew regarding the following aspects of Mapai involvement with American Jewry: reports to America on events in Eretz Israel by representatives of Mapai (1931); relations with American Zionist youth movements (1939, 1941, 1943); and maintaining Mapai influence and fund raising in the United States (1937, 1942, 1943, 1945), especially in view of the Revisionist leanings of such leaders as Abba Hillel Silver (September-October, 1945).

Among persons figuring prominently in documents are Dov Hos, Israel Merem"insky (Merom), Eliezer Kaplan, Golda Myerson (Meir), David Ben Gurion, Moshe Shertok (Sharett), Yehudit Simhoni, and Abba Hillel Silver.

Of special interest is a 37-page protocol (September 12, 1939) in which David Ben Gurion stresses the need of American Zionism for guidance from Eretz Israel and David Remez advocates sending Dov Hos to work with American Jewish youth.

Collection catalogued by repository.

Research access by consent of archivist. Photocopies provided.

SA 5/82

MASLIANSKY, ZVI HIRSCH, 1856-1943

(Born in Byelorussia; active in Hibbat Zion Movement; immigrated to United States in 1895; eloquent and influential Yiddish orator, who popularized Zionism among Yiddish-speaking immigrants to the United States.)

4 items, covering years 1896, 1908, 1918 and 1924, in Record Group V. 1282.

In Jewish National and University Library, Jerusalem.

Items include material dealing with attendance by Masliansky at the Zionist "Jahreskonferenz" in Cologne in 1908 (File 137) and a donation by Masliansky to the Palestine Restoration Fund in 1918 (File 174). Individuals in the correspondence include Judah L. Magnes, Harry Friedenwald and Stephen S. Wise.

Of interest is a letter in Hebrew (April 14, 1896) from Menahem Ussishkin in Ekaterinslaw (southern Russia) to Masliansky in New York mentioning rumors in New York and Chicago of Zionists having purchased land on the east bank of the Jordan (File 7).

Also included is a letter in Hebrew to Masliansky (7 Tishrei 5685 [1924]) from Boris Schatz relating the financial difficulties of the Bezalel Arts and Crafts School as he plans to bring an exhibition to America and spend six months raising funds for the school (File 221).

Collection catalogued by repository.

Research access not restricted. Photocopies provided.

SK 3/82

MEROM (MEREMINSKY), ISRAEL, 1891-1976

(Born in Poland; emigrated to Eretz Israel in 1924; Histadrut emissary to American Jewish labor groups and Histadrut representative in America, 1928-1945.)

Ca. 6 boxes, covering years 1928-1933, 1939-1945, interspersed in Israel Merom papers.

In Hakibbutz Hameuhad Archives, Ramat Efal, Ramat Gan.

Collection includes personal working notes, correspondence, reports, outlines of speeches, newsclippings, contracts and financial reports, minutes of meetings, contribution forms and bulletins pertaining to Merom's activities in the United States on behalf of the Histadrut. Correspondents include Golda Myerson (Meir) and David Remez, at that time members of the Histadrut executive committee, and other leaders and institutions in America and Eretz Israel. Most of the material is in Hebrew or Yiddish; some of the Yiddish documents have been translated into Hebrew by the repository.

Materials deal with the following subjects:

immigration to Eretz Israel—criteria, pioneer farm-training, activities of Hechalutz, Hashomer Hatzair, and other Jewish youth movements;

meetings and speeches during Merom's visits in various American Jewish communities;

conventions and other activities of American Jewish organizations and institutions, including the American Jewish Congress, the United Palestine Appeal, the Zionist Organization of America, the Revisionists, Poalei Zion, Workmen's Circle, Farband, the Jewish Agency, HIAS, Hadassah, and Pioneer Women; correspondents included Robert Szold, Morris Rothenberg, Louis Lipsky, Nahum Goldmann and David Pinski;

Histadrut campaigns in the United States and efforts to establish the League for Jewish Labor in Palestine;

campaigns and activities in the United States to rescue European Jewry during World War II for settlement in Eretz Israel;

relations with the American Federation of Labor (AFL) and Congress of Industrial Organizations (CIO) and their respective presidents William Green and Philip Murray, especially the former, and their diplomatic efforts on behalf of a Jewish Commonwealth in Eretz Israel; and

question of partition as debated in the United States, the United Nations and the Jewish Agency.

Of special interest are the following:

an undated report of the refusal by Eleanor Roosevelt to grant
a request by Misrachi Women for her to publish a letter protesting the British White Paper of 1939; and

report of a letter (July 7, 1933) to David Ben Gurion from
Louis D. Brandeis criticizing the Histadrut for using its power
to control others and for lacking the flexibility to attract
outsiders.

The collection also includes correspondence and other documents pertaining to the following:

Am Oved Publishing House and *Davar* (daily newspaper) con-
tracts with Jewish writers Zalman Shneour, Abraham Regelson,
Isaac Bashevis Singer, Hayim Greenberg, Ephraim Lisitzky,
Jacob Lestschinsky, David Pinski, Menahem Boraisha and
Simon Halkin, concerning the translation of their books into
Hebrew or English;

Am Oved translation and publishing business with American
publishers;

articles and items from the United States for publication in
Davar;

a request by Moshe Halevi in 1943 to raise funds in the United
States for the Ohel Theater; and

American funds toward establishing mechanical, chemical and
industrial classes at Amal High School.

Collection uncatalogued.
Research access not restricted. Photocopies provided.

TG 9/81

MEROM (MEREMINSKY), MAY BERE, 1894-
(American trained pioneer school psychologist; born in Canada;
arrived in Eretz Israel 1929; representative of Moetzet Hapoalot to
the Pioneer Women Organization in Canada and United States 1939-
1942.)
Ca. 12 items, covering years 1943-1945, in special folders among
Dr. Merom's private papers.
In the home of Dr. May Bere-Merom, 18 Zeitlin Street, Tel Aviv.

Collection includes preliminary and final reports, minutes of meetings, family background reports and summary of the unpublished research conducted at Bet Hayeled School in New York, 1943-1945, coordinated by Dr. Bere-Merom and entitled "The Effect of Bicultural Education on the Personality of the Young Child." Among the issues examined were the effect of family identification with Zionism and Eretz Israel (home background varying from ultra-Orthodox to interfaith marriage) on the children's attitude toward Eretz Israel and the effect of Hebrew/Eretz Israel content in the school on the personality of the child and his identity as an American. This research and its methods of studying children were used by Dr. Bere-Merom in her subsequent work in Israel.
Collection uncatalogued.
Research access by permission of Dr. May Bere-Merom.

TG 8/81

MILNER, ALFRED, FIRST VISCOUNT, 1854-1925
(Member of War Cabinet 1916-1918; drafted final version of the Balfour Declaration; Secretary of State for the Colonies 1919-1921.)
Ca. 100 items, covering years 1917-1919, 1922, interspersed in Milner (Papers) deposit.
In Bodleian Library, Oxford.

Collection contains miscellaneous papers of Milner relating to Palestine during the period December, 1917-March, 1918, including a statement by the Zionist Organization of America regarding Palestine, February 3, 1919; notes on Zionism, February 6, 1919 (Folder 140; remainder of deposit should be examined for further references to United States—Palestine involvement).

Another item consists of a description in Milner's diary (March 23, 1922) of his visit to Petah Tikva: "The Packing Factory recently established by an American is a very important feature in the economic life of the place . . ." (Folder 99).
Collection catalogued by repository; index of correspondents; copy in *National Register of Archives*.
Research access not restricted, but admission as reader required. Photocopies provided.

VL 5/82

MYER, HENRY DENNIS, 1882-1964
(Officer in Jewish Battalions of Royal Fusiliers, 1917-1919.)
Ca. 5 items, covering years 1918-1919, in Record Group AJ 14.
In Anglo-Jewish Archives, University College, London.

Items consist of typescript excerpts from letters by Myer to his wife referring to American Jewish volunteers attached to his 40th Battalion, Royal Fusiliers which embarked August 15, 1918 for the Palestine campaign (pp. 3; 5; 6). On February 9, 1919 after the campaign, he mentions visiting the American Zionist doctor, Schreibmann, and his Palestinian wife.
Collection not catalogued.
Research access not restricted. Photocopies provided.

VL 6/82

NADAV (HALPERN), ZVI, 1891-1959
(Engineer; one of the founders of Hashomer; early settler of Degania and Merhavia.)
1 item dated 1937, in Record Group 5/1.
In Yad Yitzhak Ben Zvi, Jerusalem.
Item consists of an article by Norman Bentwich in the *New Judea* (December, 1937) on the attitude of Felix Warburg toward Eretz Israel and his activities on its behalf (Folder 2/50).
Collection catalogued by repository.
Research access not restricted. Photocopies provided.

AF 4/82

NAMIER, LEWIS BERNSTEIN, 1888-1960
(Born near Warsaw; served in various departments of the British Foreign Office; historian, diplomat and active Zionist; political secretary of the Jewish Agency, 1929-1931 and political adviser 1938-1945; knighted 1952.)
5 items, covering years 1928, 1929, 1933, 1940, 1944, in Record Group A 312.
In Central Zionist Archives, Jerusalem.

Folder 55 of the collection contains the following correspondence and memorandum between Namier and his Zionist and non-Zionist associates:

a letter to Namier in 1928 mentioning American funding of a project for development of Haifa Bay and harbor and commencement of work on the Rockefeller Museum;

a letter to Namier from William Rosenwald of Philadelphia, Pennsylvania, dated May 21, 1929, expressing lack of personal sympathy for Zionism, but understanding of Namier's Zionist feelings;

a 2-1/2-page memorandum to Namier from Colonel Newcombe entitled "Arab Cooperation and Palestine", dated November 2, 1940, mentioning a warning by Chaim Weizmann of the effects of the White Paper on Zionists and non-Zionists in America; Jews "would use their influence against Great Britain in the press and elsewhere, now and after the war, even turning America against Britain"; and

a letter to Namier regarding a Weizmann volume being published by American friends.

There is also a letter mentioning Louis Ginzberg of the Jewish Theological Seminary of America as a member of the committee established to place German refugee teachers at the Hebrew University in 1933.

Collection catalogued by repository.

Research access not restricted. Photocopies provided.

SH 6/81

NEW ZIONIST ORGANIZATION (NZO), PRESIDENCY, LONDON

(London executive of the Zionists-Revisionists who, under Zev Jabotinsky, seceded from the World Zionist Organization in 1933 to establish the NZO; transferred to New York in 1940.)

Ca. 26 items, covering years 1940-1944, interspersed in Record Group G 4.

In Jabotinsky Institute in Israel, Tel Aviv.

Collection includes correspondence between the London executive and the American delegation of the NZO regarding the establishment of a Jewish Army (Folders 4/10; 27/2); news, information and a series of articles by A. Abraham on his trip to Eretz Israel sent in 1944 for publication in America (Folder 4/3).

Correspondents include Aharon Kopelowicz, Benjamin Akzin and Eliyahu Ben Horin.

Of special interest is a "strictly confidential" report (September, 1940) by Benjamin Akzin regarding the attempt to call a conference of all Jewish organizations for achieving unity in Zionism in order to face the world crisis and meetings between Mizrachi leaders Gedalia Bublick and Leon Gellman and NZO representatives to negotiate this possibility (Folder 27/2).

Collection catalogued by repository.

Research access not restricted. Photocopies provided.

TG 2/81

NEW ZIONIST ORGANIZATION (NZO), PRESIDENCY, UNITED STATES DELEGATION
(New York office of Zionists-Revisionists who, led by Zev Jabotinsky, seceded from the World Zionist Organization in 1933 to form the NZO; executive office transferred from London to New York in 1940.)
Ca. 880 items, covering years 1940-1944, interspersed in Record Group G5.
In Jabotinsky Institute in Israel, Tel Aviv.

Collection includes pamphlets, programs, constitution, correspondence, minutes of meetings, resolutions, application drafts, lists, press releases, newsclippings and articles about the following NZO activities:

Efforts by NZO to muster the support of American Jewry for the reconstitution of Eretz Israel as a Jewish state on both sides of the Jordan River (Folder 1/1).

Establishment of Aliyah Ltd. as a financial organ to aid refugees in reaching Eretz Israel; political efforts to gain refugees free immigration to Eretz Israel and in some cases to the United States (Folders 1/2-4,6; 3/1,7,8; 4/1,9,12,15; 5/1,3).

Formation of a Jewish army to fight with the Allied Forces in World War II: fund raising, lectures, campaigns, meetings and discussions with American officials, congressmen and senators (e.g., Henry C. Lodge, F. Condert and Gerald Nye), and others, including promotion of a meeting for a Jewish Army that took place in Manhattan on June 19, 1940 with the participation of Zev Jabotinsky, John Henry Patterson and others (Folder 1/6,7; 2; 3/2,8; 4/1,5,7,8,13; 5/2,5-7).

Zionews—the Revisionist bulletin—and the *American Jewish Chronicle* edited by Benjamin Akzin as organs to foster objectives of the NZO and requests to the editor to publish articles on the Jewish Army, Jewish State, refugees and immigration and to protest discrimination by the Joint Distribution Committee against refugee Jewish journalists espousing Revisionist attitudes (Folders 2/12; 3/4; 4/1).

Intrigues of Peter Bergson to overthrow the NZO presidency (Folder 4/14); transfer of the NZO presidency to New York in 1940; and efforts to persuade Jacob Schiff to support the NZO against the World Zionist Organization (Folders 2/5; 4/2,3,10).

Discrimination in the distribution of Zionist funds (Folder 5/4).

Death of Zev Jabotinsky during a visit to the Betar camp near New York described in a letter (August 5, 1940) to his wife Joanna (Folder 5/8); correspondence regarding funeral and memorial ceremonies, letters of condolence from various individuals and organizations in the United States (Folders 5/8-10).

Of special interest in the collection is a letter (May 7, 1940) to Benjamin Akzin from Felix Frankfurter, stating that he must refuse the request to meet with Jabotinsky and Akzin because as a judge of the Supreme Court he keeps himself insulated from anything that even remotely may come within the range of controversial public issues (Folder 4/12).

Collection catalogued by repository.

Research access not restricted. Photocopies provided.

TG 12/81

NILI

(Secret pro-British intelligence organization operating in Syria and Palestine under Turkish rule in 1915-1917 during World War I; among its leaders were Aaron, Sarah and Alexander Aaronsohn.)

5 items, covering years 1919-1922, interspersed in Record Group K2.

In Jabotinsky Institute in Israel, Tel Aviv.

Collection includes two articles by Alexander Aaronsohn about the Zionist Organization of America (ZOA), the leadership of Louis D. Brandeis and criticism of Chaim Weizmann; letters of condolence on the death of Aaron Aaronsohn from American agricultural expert David Fairchild to Felix Frankfurter and from William Bullitt in Vermont to Alexander Aaronsohn; a letter from Alexander Aaronsohn

in 1922, founder and president of the B'nai Binyamin organization, to the Histadrut Central Committee about ZOA and establishment of the Friends of B'nai Binyamin, aimed at awakening the concern and aid of American youth for the youth of Eretz Israel (Folders 6/2; 7/1-2).
Collection catalogued by repository.
Research access not restricted. Photocopies provided.

TG 2/82

PALESTINE EXPLORATION FUND (PEF), EXCAVATIONS
(PEF excavations and expeditions included those by Conrad Schick in Jerusalem (1886-1890); Gottlieb Schumacher in Western Palestine (1887); Flinders-Petrie, succeeded by F. J. Bliss and R. A. S. Macalister at Tel-el-Hesy and other sites (1890-1903; 1898-1900); Bliss and A. C. Dickie in Jerusalem (1894-1897); Macalister at Gezer (1902-1909); Bliss in Moab and Gilead (1895); T. E. Lawrence and Sir Leonard Woolley in Zin (1914).)
Ca. 235 items covering years 1889-1909, interspersed in Record Groups PEF/BLISS, PEF/PET, PEF/SCHICK, PEF/MACALISTER.
In Palestine Exploration Fund Archives, London.
    Collection includes correspondence regarding the following aspects of America PEF excavations in Eretz Israel:

> excavations by Frederick James Bliss at Tel-el-Hesy and other sites and his departure from London in 1900 (Folders PEF/BLISS; PEF/SCHICK/85,86,93,95,107,128,170);
> list (May 12, 1890) by Flinders-Petrie of objects carried to England by Dr. Camden Cobern of the United States (Folder PEF/PET/15);
> references to excavations by Selah Merrill and a description by Merrill of difficulties with Schick (Folders SCHICK/53,54,55; see also Of special interest below); and
> offer of help (December 14, 1901) by Professor Mitchell of the new American School of Archeology in Jerusalem (Folder MACALISTER/39); criticism by R. A. S. Macalister of the Spafford American Colony in Jerusalem, describing unauthorized visit to his excavations at Gezer by "a communistic American colony of religious cranks established at Jerusalem" (June

17, 1905) and their acquisition of Nablus bronzes (January 1, 1909) (Folders MACALISTER/191 and MACALISTER/295).

Of special interest:

letter (August 11, 1891) to George Armstrong, PEF executive secretary, from Selah Merrill, asking for help for his own excavations in Jerusalem and sending a private note about the experience of the young Frederick James Bliss (Folder SCHICK/ 33/1-3);
letter (November 3, 1891) to Armstrong from Schick, as PEF correspondent supporting application by Selah Merrill for PEF funding for proposed excavations at the Augustinian monastery on the eastern slope of Mount Zion (Folder SCHICK/40); and
letter (January 2, 1892) in which Schick thanks PEF for £15 for Merrill excavation fund and asks whether "he should attempt to excavate around the Al-Aksa Mosque . . ." (Folder SCHICK/46).

Collection catalogued by repository.
Catalogue/calendar in *National Register of Archives* (NRA 16370).
Research access not restricted. Photocopies not provided.

VL 6/82

PALESTINE EXPLORATION FUND (PEF), WESTERN SURVEY OF PALESTINE
(Founded in 1865 to investigate archeology, topography, geology, manners and customs of the Holy Land; sponsored various reconnaissance surveys and excavations in Eretz Israel 1865-1871; conducted surveys in western and eastern Palestine, the latter replacing the American survey stopped by the Turks.)
Ca. 32 items, covering years 1864-1880, interspersed in Record Group PEF/WS.
In Palestine Exploration Fund Archives, London.
    Collection includes correspondence among the staff of PEF Survey of Western Palestine regarding the following aspects of its relationship to the American Palestine Exploration Society (APES) Survey of Eastern Palestine.

reports on progress of E. L. Steever and the APES party (Folders WS/DRA/29, March 12, 1873; WS/DRA/25, March 25, 1873; WS/39, April 17, 1873; WS/52, August 17, 1873; WS/CON/123, January 26, 1875; WS/CON/202, December 23, 1875); dwindling of the American expedition and dissension between Steever and M. W. Shapiro (Folder WS/68, February 24, 1874); return to the United States of author Henry Van Dyke from the American party (Folder WS/82, October 21, 1875);

publication or receipt of map sheets of the American survey (Folders WS/45, January 9, 1873; WS/172, December 3, 1878; WS/191, March 28, 1879; WS/192, March 29, 1879; WS/194, April 10, 1879; WS/195, April 12, 1879; WS/197, March 15, 1879; WS/199);

fixing of boundaries between PEF and APES surveys (Folders WS/CON/51, June 19, 1873);

purchase of instruments for the American party (Folders WS/394, February 13, 1873; WS/46, June 12, 1873);

criticism that the American Survey "cannot be considered more than a mere reconnaissance" (Folder WS/CON/439, February 12, 1880); and

Selah Merrill, later U.S. Consul in Jerusalem, as archeologist of APES party (Folders WS/83, November 27, 1875; WS/89, January 20, 1876; see Of special interest below).

Correspondents include PEF Western Survey staff members Claude Conder, C. F. Tyrwhitt Drake and H. H. Kitchener; PEF London administrators George Grove, Walter Besant, J. D. Grace and George Armstrong; APES officials and staff members N. C. White, E. L. Steever and Selah Merrill.

Of special interest are the following:

Letter (January 14, 1864) from Walter Besant to Reverend Dr. Bodington in Long Island, on a proposal for a survey west of the Jordan River and suggestion for a complementary survey east of the Jordan River by an American party (Folder WS/383).

Letter (January 24, 1872) to Walter Besant from Claude Conder in Haifa on the "American movements" as requested by the PEF committee. "No one but Mr. Payne and Lieutenant Steever have appeared" and they "are quite uncertain as to what they mean to do" (Folder WS/CON/34).

Letter (February 3, 1873) to Besant from Conder evaluating Steever and his progress; plan and direction of the American party's work; M. W. Shapiro and his relationship to the work (Folder WS/CON/36).

Letter (ca. October/November 1875) to Besant from Conder (in England after rioting in Safed temporarily stopped Western Survey), comparing the extensive use of animals and baggage by the Americans with the more economical use by the British; criticism of American lack of accuracy and economy (Folder WS/82).

Letter (November 27, 1875) to Besant from Selah Merrill in Beirut about starting a journal on Palestine (Folder WS/83).

Letter (December 23, 1875) to Besant from Merrill in Beirut regarding the temporary lull in work due to the departure from the American party of James C. Lane (chief engineer), Randolph Meyer (assistant engineer) and Harvey Treat; Merrill asks Besant not to mention in writing Lane's going to New York since it may insult them (WS/84).

Letter (November 30, 1876) to George Grove from Eldridge, British Consul General in Beirut, criticizing Merrill and the organization by Americans of their expeditions (Folder WS/120).

Letter (ca. August 1877) to Besant from H. H. Kitchener concerning departure of the Americans from the country; concern by the "Beyrout Americans" (presumably of the American College) over their lack of success (Folder WS/KIT/38).

Letter (undated) to Besant from Kitchener, comparing the American and British survey sheets on areas east and west of the Jordan River, presumably when joining of PEF and APES sheets was proposed in 1878. According to Kitchener the American Survey was "an ordinary military road reconnaissance sketch" and not a survey; letter details inaccuracies in longitude and latitude saying "the map of the country to the east of the Jordan is merely the result of the iteration of a few routes, it would be unwise to expend a very large sum in its reproduction, when we may reasonably hope that a correct survey will be made at no distant date" (WS/KIT/68).

Collection catalogued by repository.

Catalogue/calendar in *National Register of Archives* (NRA 16370).

Research access not restricted. Photocopies not provided.

VL 6/82

PATTERSON, JOHN HENRY, 1867-1947
(Colonel in the British Army; commanding officer of the Zion Mule Corps in the Gallipoli campaign and later of the Jewish Legion in the Palestine campaign during World War I.)
Ca. 100 items, covering years 1940-1947, interspersed and in special folders in Record Group P177.
In Jabotinsky Institute in Israel, Tel Aviv.

Collection includes letters, telegrams, newsclippings and drafts of articles and letters regarding Colonel Patterson's activities on behalf of establishing a Jewish Army during World War II and British and American attitudes toward Zionism as reflected in the American Jewish press. Correspondents include Benzion Netanyahu, Morris Mendelson and Elias Gilner (Ginsburg) regarding Revisionist Zionist activities in the United States.

Of special interest are the following:

a draft of a letter (August 15, 1946) by Patterson to the President of the United States, requesting his intervention to alter British policy toward Jewish immigrants attempting to enter Palestine; and

letters from Congressmen Will Rogers, Jr., Andrew Schiffler and James Fulbright, dated February 25 and 29, 1944, expressing their sympathy with Patterson's request for their support of Resolutions 418 and 419 introduced in the House of Representatives. Will Rogers declared that the White Paper must be abrogated, Jewish immigration opened and a Jewish State established in Palestine (in folder labeled "Correspondence with American Politicians").

Collection catalogued by repository.
Research access not restricted. Photocopies provided.

TG 12/81

PLUGOTH HAAVODA (WORK BRIGADES) OF BETAR
1 item, dated 1933, in Record Group B5.
In Jabotinsky Institute in Israel, Tel Aviv.

Folder 3/11 contains a copy of a letter regarding the obligations of Betar immigrants from America to serve the work brigades in Eretz Israel.
Collection catalogued by repository.
Research access not restricted. Photocopies provided.

SA 1/82

RADLER-FELDMANN, YEHOSHUA, 1880-1957
(Born in Zborov, Galicia; Hebrew journalist and teacher; arrived in Eretz Israel in 1907; active in Mizrachi Party after World War I; editor of *Ha-Hed*, 1926-1953; founding member of Brit Shalom Association advocating a bi-national state for Arabs and Jews; wrote under pen name Rabbi Binyamin.)
Ca. 60 items, covering years 1940-1948, in Record Group A 357.
In Central Zionist Archives, Jerusalem.

Collection contains a special folder of statements and tributes to Judah L. Magnes, mostly in Hebrew, by Alexander Dushkin, Joseph Klausner, Norman Bentwich, Leo Baeck and others, citing his contribution to Jewish institutions and organizations in the United States and Eretz Israel (Folder 161).

Also includes correspondence, newspaper and magazine articles, and minutes of meetings in Hebrew, English and Yiddish, regarding American Zionist financial aid in raising the social and economic status of women in Eretz Israel via the Federation of Zionist Women in the United States as reported by Deborah Feldman (Folder 8); the American response and/or support for Rabbi Binyamin's articles, speeches and activities toward improving Arab-Jewish relations and the Brit Shalom Association (Folders 25; 47); lectures, articles and correspondence encouraging efforts by American Jewry against Nazi terror and genocide and on behalf of admitting survivors to Eretz Israel, and the Al Domi rescue organization (Folders 49; 77; 99; 143; 144).
Collection catalogued by repository.
Research access not restricted. Photocopies provided.

SG 12/81

REZNIK (HAROZEN), JACOB, 1899-1977
(Israeli teacher, historian and archivist.)
1 item, dated 1894, in Record Group A 335.

In Central Zionist Archives, Jerusalem.

Folder 8 of the collection includes a two-page handwritten report in Hebrew of a meeting of the local French Palestine Committee on 4 Tishri 5654 (October 4, 1894) sent to "Le Grand Rabbin du Consistoire Contrale des Israelites du France," discussing negotiations and details of the purchase for 60,000 francs of 20,000 dunams of land near Nahalat Golan in the Bashan [for Bnai Yehuda] by the Rumanian association on behalf of the American and English associations of Hovevei Zion.

Collection catalogued by repository.

Research access not restricted. Photocopies provided.

SG 9/81

ROSOFF, ISRAEL, 1896-1948
(Active Zionist in Russia and Eretz Israel; emissary of the NZO to the United States after World War II.)

Ca. 19 items, covering years 1917, 1945-1946, interspersed in Record Group P 200.

In Jabotinsky Institute in Israel, Tel Aviv.

File 8/1 of this collection includes correspondence with American Jewish leaders including Louis D. Brandeis, Stephen S. Wise and Abba Hillel Silver regarding Zionist affairs and their attitudes toward the political situation in Eretz Israel; correspondence with Samuel Merlin and Paul Delogatz regarding the American League for a Free Palestine; and a list of guests attending a reception held by Senator and Mrs. Guy M. Gillette honoring Israel Rosoff at the Hebrew Committee for National Liberation on January 15, 1946.

See well, p. 14.

Of special interest is a letter (January 28, 1946) to Rosoff from William O'Dwyer, mayor of New York, stating that the people of New York will continue to support the Jewish people in their hopes "to settle in Palestine as a haven of refuge, a place where they could build a new life without restrictions."

Collection catalogued by repository.

Research access not restricted. Photocopies provided.

TG 12/81

RUPPIN, ARTHUR, 1876-1943
(Father of Zionist settlement in Eretz Israel; born in Germany; settled in Eretz Israel before World War I; economist and sociologist.)

6 items, dated 1922, in Record Group S 55.
In Central Zionist Archives, Jerusalem.

The collection includes correspondence between Ruppin and Louis Lipsky. One letter mentions Adolph Ochs' impressions of Zionist activities in Eretz Israel following a trip there and his decision to open the columns of the *New York Times* to articles on Zionism (Folder 258).
Collection catalogued by repository.
Research access not restricted. Photocopies provided.

DF 11/81

SACHER, HARRY, 1881-1971
(Active British Zionist, lawyer, author and journalist; member of the Zionist Executive, 1927-1931.)
Ca. 11 items, covering years 1931, 1944-1945, interspersed in Record Group A 289.
In Central Zionist Archives, Jerusalem.

Collection includes copies of manuscripts for newspaper articles, book reviews and statements about American Zionist leaders Henrietta Szold and Louis D. Brandeis and about the potential American political and social contributions to Eretz Israel in preparation for the establishment of a Jewish commonwealth (Folders 66 and 75).

Of special interest is a 2-1/2-page statement (March, 1946) entitled "The Meaning of Zionism" prepared by Martin Buber for the Anglo-American Committee of Inquiry, tracing the historical roots of Zionism and emphasizing the necessity for open immigration and self-determination of the Jewish community in its national homeland (Folder 103).
Collection catalogued by repository.
Research access not restricted. Photocopies provided.

SH 6/81

SAFRIEL (PISAREVSKY), YESHAYAHU, 1884-1971
(Born in Ukraine; active Zionist also in London and Berlin; settled in Eretz Israel 1932; secretary of the anti-partitionist Committee for an Undivided Palestine and editor of its bulletin, *Eretz Habehirah* 1936-1938.)
Ca. 34 items, covering years 1929, 1937-1938, in Record Group A 294.

In Central Zionist Archives, Jerusalem.

Collection contains material regarding the Committee for an Undivided Palestine and leadership of the World Zionist Organization.

Files 11-14 include correspondence, minutes of meetings, bulletins, newsclippings and speeches of the Committee for an Undivided Palestine, which opposed the partition of Eretz Israel and disseminated anti-partitionist literature to gain American support during 1937-1938. Among the correspondents from America, where Jewish sentiment against partition predominated, were Robert Szold, Rose Jacobs, Emanuel Neumann and Chaim Tchernowitz. Special folder 10/8/6 in File 14 contains newsclippings in Hebrew, English and Yiddish from the American press (e.g., *Der Morgen Journal* and *Opinion*) as well as pamphlets and addresses opposing partition.

Of special interest are the following:

> a 5-page address by Robert Szold, entitled "The Proposed Partition of Palestine," to the Hadassah Convention in October, 1937 (Folder 14/10/8/6);
> *Eretz Habehirah, Bulletin of the Anti-partitionists*, Nos. 1-3, with articles by Rose Jacobs and Meir Berlin among others and reports of anti-partitionist activity in the United States (Folder 14/10/8/6);
> a 16-page pamphlet entitled "Partition or Zionism: the Fate of Palestine and the National Jewish Homeland," by Abraham Revusky, published May, 1938 by the Zionist Committee for an Undivided Palestine (Folder 14/10/8/6); and
> a 2-letter exchange (March 28 and April 1, 1929) between Jacob De Haas and Samuel Landman of the London *Jewish Chronicle* discussing leadership of the World Zionist Organization and Stephen S. Wise declining the presidency of the WZO (Folder 6).

Collection catalogued by repository.
Research access not restricted. Photocopies provided.

SG 10/81

SAMUEL, EDWIN HERBERT, SECOND VISCOUNT, 1898-1978
(Son of the first High Commissioner of Palestine; officer in the British Colonial Services; principal of the Institute of Public Administration in Jerusalem.)

Ca. 75 items, covering years 1931-1945, interspersed in Record Group 103.

In Israel State Archives, Jerusalem.

Correspondence includes letters mentioning the visit to Palestine in 1944 of Reverend Waitskill H. Sharp of the Unitarian Church (Folder 655/28); the United States listed among countries where applications are pending for immigration to Palestine for the period May 1, 1939 to September 30, 1939 (Folder 656/35); and efforts in 1938/39 by Mary Lyons to place an article about "Krite" (Krith), a "very American" Hashomer Hatzair group stationed at Hadar in the Sharon plain, in an American magazine (Folder 655/23).

The collection also includes the following:

Correspondence with Henrietta Szold; Edward Erich, Felix and Giselle Warburg; Chaim Arlosoroff and Mordechai Ben Tov regarding Zionist affairs (Folders 655/14; 655/16; 655/24; 655/25; 658/8).

Minutes and correspondence of the Jewish-Arab Relations Committee (JARC) in the United States, donations to which were to be divided between Brit Shalom, the Jewish Agency and the Labor Organization. Included is a letter from Henrietta Szold acknowledging her agreement with the objectives of Brit Shalom, but her inability to align herself with any political propaganda group (1931- Folder 658/8).

Correspondence thanking Samuel or congratulating him for various appointments and publications, from David de Sola Pool, Nathan Straus and Edward Warburg (1931/33- Folder 655/16; 1939/40- Folder 655/24).

Reference to the impact of American press, public opinion, domestic economic policy and "imperial" interests cited by John B. Glubb and others from the Chief Secretary's Office in response to Samuel's "Balance of Forces" (1945- Folder 657/7).

Reports, minutes of meetings, letter and newsclippings regarding the Anglo-American Committee of Inquiry; aims, members and testimony by Chaim Weizmann (1946- Folder 657/16).

Expressions of support for partition by Norman L. Corwin (1947/48- Folder 655/33).

Samuel urging Chaim Arlosoroff to meet Walter Rogers of the Institute of Current World Affairs established by Charles Crane in New York (1930/31- Folder 655/14).

There are also references to the following fundraising activities:

the Carnegie Foundation urged by Samuel to interest the Inter-racial Council in America in providing some financial support for Brit Shalom and an appeal to 60 rabbis of the Reform movement in America to support Brit Shalom (Folders 135/I,II,III-early 1930s);

funding of a laboratory at the Hebrew University discussed with Tamar de Sola Pool; Judah Magnes approached for money from the Blymauer Fund and regarding a donation by Samuel to a fund in memory of Reuben Staller (1937/38- Folder 655/21); and

discouraging the dispatch of [Gershon] Schocken to America to investigate the fundraising process because America had reached the limit for fundraising (1939/40- Folder 655/24).

The collection also contains letters, reports and circulars regarding Samuel's activities on behalf of the Hebrew University (1938-Folder 143); request by Samuel for the opinion of Mr. Embree of the International House in New York regarding the establishment of an institute in Jerusalem to study racial problems in the Middle East (1931- Folder 658/8); and the possibility of bringing the Palestine Orchestra to America, thus assisting in raising funds for its support (1937/38- Folder 655/21).

Collection catalogued by repository.

Research access not restricted. Photocopies provided.

DF 4/82

SAMUEL, HERBERT LOUIS, FIRST VISCOUNT, 1870-1963

(British statesman and philosopher; first High Commissioner of Palestine 1920-1925.)

Ca. 14 items, covering years 1919-1948, interspersed in Record Group 1.

In Israel State Archives, Jerusalem.

Collection contains letters, newsclippings, a booklet and telegram concerning Zionist political activities in the United States and the responses they evoked:

Surprise expressed by President Woodrow Wilson to Felix Frankfurter at the necessity of reiterating his continued support for the Balfour Declaration (1919- Folder 103).

Fear of the British Foreign Office that the Arabs of Palestine would select the United States or France as the protecting power of

an Arab administration if Great Britain adhered to the Zionist program for the Palestine Mandate (1919- Folder 5).

Support by the American Jewish Congress and Zionist Organization of America (ZOA) for establishment of a Jewish Commonwealth in Palestine, including statements by Stephen S. Wise and
Jacob De Haas (1919- Folder 5).

United States support for the Zionist Organization as attested
by Lord Balfour to Samuel (1919- Folder 5).

Description by Chaim Weizmann of his 8-day tour of three
cities in the United States in 1924 reporting American readiness to
donate funds for Zionist purposes; conference called by Louis
Marshall to form an investment corporation as well as a committee
to work out a constitution and plans for the Jewish Agency and
support for Keren Hayesod; projected capability of Keren Hayesod
in America to contribute 2½-3 million dollars to Palestine in 1924
(1924- Folder 11).

Meyer Weisgal as Secretary of the ZOA expressing appreciation
for the services of Samuel as High Commissioner (1925- Folder 12).

Correspondence between Felix Warburg and Samuel on their
views about proposed partition in 1937, acknowledging that neither
position is popular in Zionist circles; American Federation of Labor
and Senator Hamilton Lewis protesting the British plan for partition
(1937- Folder 19).

Efforts by Elie Eliachar in New York in 1948 to interest Christian clergymen in the fate of Jerusalem; and a suggestion that British
forces remain in Jerusalem under British-French-American trusteeship (1948- Folder 26).

The American memorial at the Technion in honor of Frederick
Hermann Kisch is discussed in a letter from Dr. E. Chaim Alexander
to Samuel.

Collection catalogued by repository.

Research access not restricted. Photocopies provided.

DF 4/82

SCHWADRON COLLECTION OF AUTOGRAPHS AND POR-
TRAITS, EINSTEIN FILES
(Unique collection of autographs and portraits of prominent Jews
acquired by Abraham Schwadron, 1878-1957, Israel folklorist and
Hebrew writer.)
4 items, covering years 1921-1937, in Record Group 4° 1357.

In Jewish National and University Library, Jerusalem.

Collection includes letters and a pamphlet dealing mainly with Albert Einstein's interest in the establishment of the Hebrew University and fundraising efforts of American Jews (especially Solomon Rosenbloom) on behalf of the university (Files 71; 72; 74).

Of special interest is an 8-page undated (1921?) letter in the handwriting of Solomon Ginzberg, private secretary to Einstein, dealing mainly with the latter's 1921 trip to the United States together with Chaim Weizmann to promote the Hebrew University. Addressed to Solomon Rosenbloom and signed by Einstein, the letter discusses fundraising efforts in the United States on behalf of the Hebrew University, especially the library; the aim of the American Jewish Physicians Committee to raise seven million dollars for the Medical Department; and the need to found a Department of Jewish Philosophy and Religious Studies (File 74).

Collection catalogued by repository.

Research access not restricted. Photocopies provided.

SK 3/82

SELIGMAN, MAX (LAW OFFICE)
(Law firm representing members of the underground imprisoned by the British authorities in 1947-1948.)
12 items, covering years 1947-1948, in a special folder in Record Group HT 13.
In Jabotinsky Institute in Israel, Tel Aviv.

Collection includes letters and telegrams regarding Seligman's visit to the United States on behalf of the Jewish prisoners in Eretz Israel as a delegate of the Assirei Zion Committee. Correspondence mentions Samson Weiss, Abraham Unger, Samuel Margoshes, Boris Smolar, [Samuel] Rosenthal, the Chicago Chapter of the National Lawyers Guild, the United Zionists-Revisionists of America, the National Council of Young Israel and the Assirei Zion Fund (Folder 11/2).

Collection catalogued by repository.

Research access not restricted. Photocopies provided.

SA 1/82

SHEINBOIM, ELIEZER YITZHAK, 1854-1928
(Member of Hovevei Zion in Odessa; settled in Jerusalem in 1921.)

6 items, covering years 1921-1927, in Record Group V. 948.
In Jewish National and University Library, Jerusalem.

Collection includes correspondence in Hebrew with Jews in America expressing their wish to settle in Eretz Israel; parents' concern for their children in Eretz Israel (Folder 7) and congratulations on Sheinboim's safe arrival there (Folder 13).
Collection catalogued by repository.
Research access not restricted. Photocopies provided.

SK 4/82

SINGER, MENDEL, 1890-
(Born in Galicia; active in Poalei Zion; first came to Eretz Israel in 1909; settled permanently in Haifa in 1934; reporter for *Davar*.)
Ca. 23 items, covering years 1906-1935, interspersed in Record Group 15.
In Hakibbutz Hameuhad Archives, Ramat Efal, Ramat Gan.

Collection includes memoirs, newsclippings, notes and minutes of meetings, mainly in Yiddish (a few in Hebrew), relating primarily to the Poalei Zion party in America and its publication *Yiddisher Arbeter* (*Yiddisher Kemfer*).
Collection not catalogued.
Research access not restricted. Photocopies provided.

TG 10/81

SIRKIS, DANIEL, 1882-1965
(Born in Poland; settled in Eretz Israel, 1925; headed Jewish Council in Tel Aviv-Jaffa.)
15 items, covering years 1939-1943, in Record Group A 340.
In Central Zionist Archives, Jerusalem.

Collection includes letters, circulars, newspaper clippings and telegrams regarding Jewish and United States governmental pressure toward promoting Zionist aims in Eretz Israel and opposition to Chaim Weizmann suggesting at the B'nai B'rith convention in the United States (1941) that the establishment of a federation of Arab countries would help solve the problem of Eretz Israel. Correspondents include David Ben Gurion and Zev Jabotinsky (Folders 15; 20 and 1/X).
Collection catalogued by repository.
Research access not restricted. Photocopies provided.

DF 11/81

SUKENIK, ELIEZER LIPA, 1889-1953
(Born in Poland; settled in Eretz Israel, 1912; professor of archeology at the Hebrew University and director of its Museum of Jewish Antiquities.)
Ca. 188 items, covering years 1930-1947, in Record Group 11/1.
In Yad Yitzhak Ben Zvi, Jerusalem.

Collection contains correspondence dealing with Sukenik's scholarly contacts with archeologists and universities and his efforts to build up the reference library of the Museum of Jewish Antiquities of the Hebrew University, mostly by exchange with American researchers and institutions and by a lecture tour to the United States. Correspondents include Nelson Glueck, William F. Albright, G. Ernest Wright, Ralph Marcus, C. C. McCown, and other professors from American universities and Judah L. Magnes (Folders 1/4-5; 2/1-3,5-7; 3/2,4-6; 4; 8/1-5).
Of special interest are:

a booklet entitled *The American Teaching Hospital—Report of a Survey with Special Reference to Needs in Palestine*, by Dr. Eli Davis, published by the Hadassah Medical Organization (Folder 1/4); and
an exchange of 4 letters (May 22-November 23, 1947) between Sukenik and Mr. and Mrs. Mark Sugarman of New York concerning their donation of an illuminated Italian Megillah (Scroll of Esther) dating from 1616 to the library of the Museum of Jewish Antiquities at the Hebrew University (Folder 3/5).

Collection catalogued by repository.
Research access not restricted. Photocopies available.

SK 6/82

TABENKIN, YITZHAK, 1887-1971
(Zionist labor leader; born in Byelorussia; settled in Eretz Israel, 1912; among the founders of Poalei Zion, Hakibbutz Hameuhad, Ahdut Haavodah and the Histadrut.)
6 items, covering years 1912, 1934-1938, 1947, in Record Group 15.
In Hakibbutz Hameuhad Archives, Ramat Efal, Ramat Gan.

Folders 45, 51, 70 and 77 contain letters in Hebrew to Tabenkin from emissaries in the United States regarding their activities, including a complaint in 1938 that American Jewish leaders, especially Stephen S. Wise, are obstacles to Poalei Zion activities (Folder 51). Folder 54 includes a letter dated May 29, 1947 from Tabenkin to Yitzhak Ben Aharon criticizing the kibbutz delegation in the United States for its lack of enthusiasm and failure to attract young people to the movement and also suggesting the formation of an association called Friends of the Kibbutz as a means of gaining wider access to the Jewish community.

Collection catalogued by repository.

Research access not restricted. Photocopies provided.

TG 9/81

TULIN, ABRAHAM, 1882-1973

(American Zionist; delegate to Zionist Congresses; member of Executive Committee, ZOA; member of American Zionist Emergency Council; chief counsel for American Zionist organizations before Anglo-American Committee of Inquiry on the Palestine Question.)

Ca. 150 items, covering years 1921-1948, interspersed, in Record Group A 342.

In Central Zionist Archives, Jerusalem.

Collection includes correspondence, reports, newspapers, clippings and a personal notebook dealing with the following subjects:

Jewish Agency contacts with key figures in the American oil industry, including the petroleum attaché of the U.S. Department of State (Folder 39);

Activities of the Zionist Organization of America, including Tulin's candidacy for the Zionist Congress in 1929, Keren Hayesod, the American Zion Commonwealth; and of the Committee on Palestine Activities of the ZOA appointed by Julian Mack to determine activities in Eretz Israel, whose members included Stephen S. Wise, Simon Rothenberg, Horace Kallen and N. Lindheim (Folders 58; 59; 80; 101).

Ideas and opinions of Louis D. Brandeis regarding the functions and activities of the ZOA and its relationship with the World Zionist Organization (WZO) from 1929-1932 (Folder 82).

Speeches by Emanuel Neumann delivered at the 18th Zionist Congress in Prague, 1933 (Folder 57) and the American role in the Zionist Annual Conference in London, June-August 1920 (Folder 105).

American Zionist position in 1945 based on opposition to the earlier separation of Transjordan; figuring prominently in the material are U.S. Secretary of State James F. Byrnes, Abba Hillel Silver, U.S. Under Secretary of State Dean Acheson, Walter C. Lowdermilk and Milton Handler (Folders 81; 84).

Response of American Jewish leadership, United States government and American media to the emergent Jewish State in March-May 15, 1948: articles, speeches and statements by Abba Hillel Silver, Emanuel Neumann, Secretary of State George Marshall (Folder 87).

Widespread American support for Haganah in 1947-1948 (Folder 87).

Draft constitution for the Jewish State proposed by American Zionist lawyers with comments by lawyers Jacob Robinson and Will Maslow (Folder 87).

Activities of the Committee for a Jewish Army in 1942 (Folder 95).

American Zionist leaders' reactions to anti-Jewish attitudes among British Mandatory officials 1929-1931: Passfield Commission; Shaw Simpson Commission; Permanent Mandates Commission. Correspondents include Louis D. Brandeis, Julian Mack, Leon Lauterstein and Robert Szold (Folders 76; 79; 82).

U.S. Army career of Abraham Tulin in the Near East in 1919 as a captain in charge of distribution of United States Food Relief there, including Eretz Israel (Folder 66).

Book of documents of Zionist history compiled by Tulin in 1946-1947 for the Jewish Agency (Folder 66).

Of special interest are:

A copy of a 2½-page letter (April 23, 1946) from Secretary of State James F. Byrnes, denying that the separation of Transjordan violates any existing United States-British treaty (Folder 84).

Report (August 20, 1946) on a meeting of Milton Handler and Tulin with Under Secretary of State Dean Acheson regarding the recognition of Transjordan; Acheson, reporting that the American Government had presented the partition plan of the Jewish Agency to the British Government, expressed hope that the plan would be accepted by Britain and the Arabs thus obviating the consideration of the problem in the United Nations and the involvement of the USSR (Folder 84).

Letter (July 19, 1946) by Benjamin Akzin describing the visit by a representative from the legal adviser of the State Department regarding Zionist attempts to have the Grand Mufti prosecuted as a war criminal (Folder 84).

70-page personal notebook of Tulin from the Zionist Annual Conference, London (June 22-August 29, 1920) detailing all of the approximately 30 meetings he attended; the last two pages contain his personal feelings about the conference: ". . . broke hearts not by what it did but by what it failed to do" (Folder 105).

Folder 82 in its entirety: ca. 80 letters reflecting the private opinions, international stature and extensive influence of Louis D. Brandeis, e.g., memo from Julian Mack to the Mack-Brandeis group (June 14, 1930) reporting that British Foreign Secretary Arthur Henderson requested U.S. Ambassador to Britain Ronald Lindsay to seek the opinions of Brandeis on the situation in Palestine.

The collection also includes reports by four American Jews who visited Eretz Israel in the 1920s (Folder 70);

> Isidore M. Nobel (May, 1921) contrasts the general inefficiency of the Zionist Commission with the fine work of Hadassah;
> Emanuel M. Mohl (February, 1921) includes a report on the sale of American Zion Commonwealth shares;
> Solomon Rosenbloom reports (March, 1922) to the Palestine Development Council on the thriving colonists in Petah Tikvah, Rehovot, Gedera and Ekron, despite difficult conditions and lack of adequate support by American Jews; and
> Harry Fischel, New York builder and philanthropist, met [in early 1920s] with High Commissioner Sir Herbert Samuel, who expressed disappointment with the lack of American investments in Eretz Israel.

Also included are two letters regarding colonization efforts by American Jewish Legionnaires in Eretz Israel 1929-1930 (Folder 82).

The collection also contains correspondence, a cablegram, reports and newsletters regarding publicity and fundraising by the American Society for the Technion (Folders 38-39), covering the following subjects: an appeal by the society to engineers and leaders of technical industrial enterprises in the United States for the furtherance of engineering education, vocational training and industrial

for samples from Turkish archives see pp 153 — 161

development in Eretz Israel; the Kisch Memorial Laboratory; donation of the Leon Solomon Moissieff Library to the Technion through
the American Palestine Engineers. Correspondents and/or supporters
include Albert Einstein, General Bernard Montgomery, Frieda Schiff
Warburg and Frederick H. Kisch.

Of special interest is a cable (November 14, 1943) sent from
General Bernard Montgomery to Albert Einstein via General Dwight
D. Eisenhower in Algiers. Montgomery states his delight in the estab-
lishment of the Kisch Memorial Laboratory and his readiness to
accept the position of Honorary Chairman (Folder 61).
Collection catalogued by repository.
Research access not restricted. Photocopies provided.

SH 5/82

TURKEY, ARCHIVES OF THE FOREIGN OFFICE
5 items, covering years 1898 and 1913, interspersed in Record Group
DBHE.
In Ottoman State Archives, Istanbul, Turkey.

see
Mf. 3F
153

Collection includes letters, memos, reports and newsclippings
sent by Ali Ferruh, Ottoman Minister in Washington, D.C., and
Abraham Farhi, Ottoman Consul General in Boston, to the Ottoman
Minister for Foreign Affairs and to the Yildiz Palace, Istanbul, concerning the appointment of Oscar Straus as Minister to Turkey, early
activities of U.S. Jews on behalf of Zionism and attempts by these
Ottoman officials to combat Zionism in the United States.

Of special interest are the following:

Letter from Ferruh, in French (May 12, 1898), concerning the
May 10-11 conference to which Ferruh sent a "secret agent";
Mehemed A. R. Webb, head of the Moslem community in New York,
received information from Richard Gottheil that postponement was
due to the Spanish American War and the conference would not
reconvene for the duration of hostilities (File DBHE 332/17, no.
9557/66).

Newsclipping of article (June 14, 1898) from The World, entitled "Turkey Frowns on Free Palestine"; reporting Ferruh's reaction
to the recent meeting in New York of 5,000 "Friends of the Ghetto";
his belief that Jews in Palestine and Turkey are happy and contented
and that such Zionist agitation can be harmful; his remark that the
Zionist movement "has attracted a great deal of attention throughout

Europe and has developed into one of the forces in [world] politics"
(File DBHE 332/17).

Newsclipping (June 14, 1898) from *The Sun*, entitled "Scheme
to Colonize Palestine: The Turkish Minister on the Movement of the
'Friends of the Ghetto' ": comments by Ferruh on the conference
held at the Spanish and Portuguese Synagogue in New York by the
"Friends of the Ghetto," whose object "was to colonize Palestine
by Jewish immigration and to make the Holy Land again a land of
promise for the Israelites," which concerned Turkish sovereignty;
view of Ferruh that the Jews enjoyed a favorable and prosperous
status throughout the Ottoman Empire (File DBHE 332/17).

Newsclipping of article (June 17, 1898) from the *Jewish Messenger* supporting the position of Ferruh: "but will his statement be
effectual in restoring to sanity those whose zeal outruns their discretion, and who, under the mask of protection, may be accelerating a
catastrophe that may dwarf mediaeval holocausts?"; "the great body
of Israelites in America and Europe have no sympathy with Zionism
and a Jewish State"; hopes that the minister will have an influence
on "our Don Quixotes" (File DBHE 332/17).

"A memorandum on the relations between the Ottoman government and the Zionist administration," a statement of principles
submitted to the Action Committee and the Zionist Congress in
August 1913, enclosed by Abraham Farhi in his report of August 7,
1913 to Ottoman Ministry for Foreign Affairs.

Memo opposes the Hebrew Gymnasium in Jerusalem being
placed under the protection of the French government, as reported
in *Dos Yiddische Folk* on July 11, 1913, and the use of German as
language of instruction at the Haifa Technical Institute, reported in
Hapoel Hazair on June 20, 1913 as giving color to suspicions that
Zionist institutions are being utilized to strengthen interests of
foreign governments in Palestine:

> Nothing can be more fatal to Zionist aspirations than to harbor
> distrust of the Ottoman Government and the Turkish people. The
> Ottoman Government and the Turkish people have ever shown
> themselves friendly and even magnanimous to the Jewish people . . .
> Zionist success must inevitably redound to the wealth and welfare
> of the Empire at large. . . . In short we desire to develop a Jewish
> policy in Palestine, but a policy that shall be a permanent and

beneficient Jewish province in the Ottoman Empire. This we hold to be the Zionist political ideal.

Memo signed by eight U.S. Zionists: "N. Friedman, M.D.; Jacob De Haas; Adolph Hubbard; Henry Hurwitz, M.A.; Julius Meyer, Boston, Mass.; Horace W. [sic] Kallen, Ph.D., Madison, Wis.; Boris Kazmann, Battle Creek, Mich.; Henry M. Sheffer, Ph.D., Minneapolis, Minn." (File DBHE, 332/17, no. 269).
Collection catalogued by repository.
Research access must be requested six months in advance.
See Supplement I. Photocopies provided only by request six months in advance.

MKÖ and HK 1/83

TURKEY, ARCHIVES OF THE PRIME MINISTER'S OFFICE (BASBAKANALIK ARSIVI)
7 items, covering years 1896, 1898 and 1899, interspersed in Record Group BBA, YEE.
In Ottoman State Archives, Istanbul, Turkey.

Collection includes letters, memos, reports and newsclippings sent by Ali Ferruh, Ottoman Minister in Washington, D.C., and Abraham Farhi, Ottoman Consul General in Boston to the Ottoman Minister for Foreign Affairs and to the Yildiz Palace, Istanbul, concerning the appointment of Oscar Straus as Minister to Turkey, early Zionist activities of U.S. Jews and opposition by these Ottoman officials to Zionism in the United States.

Of special interest are the following:

Memo from Ferruh in Turkish (June 15, 1896) on proposed appointment of Oscar Straus as U.S. Minister to Istanbul; apprehension that it would facilitate the promotion of Zionist propaganda; declarations by Ferruh to the press to combat Zionism (File BBA, YEE,Ç/II/85-86/54/136).

Memo from Ferruh in Turkish (April 27, 1898) discussing the "Washington Committee, a sister organization of the 'Izmir Secret Association of Judaism and Zionism,'" its membership, leadership and financial activities; subscriptions from American Jews who believe in "the idea of the Promised Land"; Richard Gottheil and Stephen S. Wise cited as New York committee leaders; recommendation by Ferruh that an agent be sent to its May 10-11 conference to learn about its organization and resolutions; suggestion to keep watch on certain Jews in Palestine (File BBA,YEE,A/II/748-49/54/136).

Memo from Ferruh in Turkish (June 23, 1898) including a positive appraisal by Ferruh of his work in influencing the American Jewish public against Zionism: "I can assure His Imperial Majesty that . . . I shattered the Palestinian dream of the Zionists which was becoming a serious question and left its supporters in desperation and sorrow"; report that the *Jewish Messenger* published his declaration and commentary concerning Zionism, including the remark: "the great body of Israelites in America and Europe have no sympathy with Zionism and a Jewish State . . ." (File BBA,YEE,Ç/II/98/54/136).

Letter from Ferruh in French (June 23, 1898) citing the nomination of Straus as an unfortunate opportunity to further Zionist goals; recommendation by Ferruh that something should be done to oppose and discourage various resolutions on Palestine passed at a recent U.S. gathering; declarations made by Ferruh to American newspapers; claims that he made favorable impression and caused decisive blow to Zionism; his views released to the *Jewish Messenger* (File BBA,YEE,Ç/II/98/36).

Memo from Ferruh in Turkish (January 24, 1899) regarding the restriction of Jews from entering Palestine by refusing them visas lest they settle there; difficulties due to U.S. State Department intervention and alteration of Ottoman policy; opinion of Ferruh that Straus is helping Zionists in Palestine and, as an "ardent supporter of the Palestine question . . . his activities should be closely scrutinized" (File BBA,YEE,Ç/II/275-276/54/136).

Letter from Ferruh in French (May 5, 1899) regarding the idea of U.S. Jews that a Jewish State can be created in Palestine through purchase of land by gathering American Jewish funds; discussion of newsclipping from *The Press* (see below); American Jews think that Turkey would be willing to weigh the idea for financial considerations, but Ferruh claims that Turkey, in good financial position, would never sell to the Zionists (File BBA,YEE,Ç/II/98/36; see below).

Newsclipping of article presumably from *The Press*, entitled "Turkey Will Not Sell Palestine," reporting that Ferruh "is deeply concerned over the prominence given in this country [United States] to the Hebrew propaganda which looks to the purchase and occupation of Palestine by a free Jewish nation"; that his government has no interest in selling "any part of its Arabian country": that he fails to understand why Americans think Jews under Turkish sovereignty should be discontented, since "the Jewish people under the Turkish Sultan are prosperous, happy and contented" (enclosure, File BBA, YEE,Ç/II/275-276/54/136).

Collection catalogued by repository.

Research access must be requested six months in advance.

See Supplement II. Photocopies provided only by request six months in advance.

MKÖ and HK 1/83

UNITED ZIONISTS-REVISIONISTS, WORLD SECRETARIAT, PARIS

Ca. 310 items covering years 1946-1948, in Record Group G 7.

In Jabotinsky Institute in Israel, Tel Aviv.

Collection includes correspondence in English, Yiddish, French, Hebrew and German between the United Zionists-Revisionists of America and the World Secretariat in Paris regarding the American Committee for Palestine's Political Prisoners (Leassirenu); Revisionist participation in the extraordinary meeting called by the American Zionist Emergency Council on February 17, 1947; the boycott of British goods in the United States to protest British policy in Eretz Israel; and the *dinar* and *shekel* campaigns and financial difficulties of the Revisionist Party in Eretz Israel and also contains a list of members of the United Zionists Revisionists in America (Folders 4/3; 7/3).

Individuals figuring prominently in these folders include David Bukspan, Benzion Netanyahu and Eliezer Shostak; institutions and/ or organizations include the Jewish National Fund, Hadassah, the Tel Hai Fund, the American Jewish Conference, and Brit Trumpeldor of America (Folder 4/3).

Collection catalogued by repository.

Research access not restricted. Photocopies provided.

SA 2/82

WEIZMANN, CHAIM, 1874-1952

(First president of the State of Israel; president of the World Zionist

Organization 1920-1930, 1935-1946; distinguished scientist.)

Ca. 100 items, covering years 1914-1920, interspersed in Record Groups 1914-1920 of the Weizmann Archives; copious relevant material in later years to appear in subsequent volumes.

In Weizmann Archives, Weizmann Institute, Rehovot.

Collection includes correspondence, reports, bulletins, speeches and other documents dealing with the following subjects:

Formation of the Provisional Executive Committee for Zionist Affairs at a special conference of U.S. Zionists held August 30, 1914 to assume responsibility for maintenance of Zionist institutions in Palestine formerly administered by the Action Committee of the World Zionist Organization (WZO), which was rendered inoperable by the war in Europe; tasks, activities, views, conventions and relations of the committee with other organizations (Files September, October 1914; March 13-31, October, December 16-31, 1915; October 18-26, November 10-15, 1917; January 27-31, March 22-25, 1918); resignation of Judah L. Magnes from the committee in protest to the Zionist Organization of America (ZOA) political definition of a Jewish national homeland in Eretz Israel, which he envisioned as a Jewish cultural center, reflected in correspondence between Magnes and Louis D. Brandeis (Files June, September, October and November 18-30, 1915).

Fund-raising, financial situation and Zionist activities of various U.S. Jewish organizations including Hadassah, American Jewish Congress, Federation of American Zionists, American Jewish Relief Committee, Mizrachi, ZOA, Poalei Zion, Order Sons of Zion, American Jewish Committee and American Committee for a Jewish Legion in reports to Weizmann (Files September 1914; May, July, October, December 16-31, 1915; January 1917; January 9-15, December 3-6, 1918; September 13-30, 1920); disagreement and competition between the American Jewish Relief Committee and ZOA (Files November 5-10, December 27-31, 1920).

U.S. Jewish leadership, its attitude toward Zionism and Eretz Israel, World War I and United States neutrality, Balfour Declaration in reports to Weizmann from Aaron Aaronsohn, Magnes, Eliyahu Lewin-Epstein and Jacob De Haas (Files September, 1914; January 7-31, 1915; December, 1916; May 14-20, December 13-17, 18-23, 1917; November 22-26, December 3-6, 13-17, 1918; January 28-31, 1919).

Requests for Weizmann's views on Zionism and other issues from various personalities and organizations in the United States; invitations for him to visit the United States and to present his views before American Jewry (Files September, December 17-31, 1914; April, 1915; January 17-22, November 1-2, December 13-17, 1918; July, October, 13-24, 1920).

Disagreement between Weizmann and Louis D. Brandeis regarding the Brandeis plan to include non-Zionists in important projects for Eretz Israel; views of Brandeis on upbuilding Eretz Israel; Brandeis-Weizmann relationship in general (Files November 1-2, 1918; July 9-18, August 27-31, September 13-30, November 5-1, 1920).

Aaron Aaronsohn praised for his good work as emissary to American Jewry, reported by Louis Brandeis and Felix Frankfurter (Files October 26-31, November 1-2, 1918).

Sympathy of President Woodrow Wilson for Zionism (Files May 14-22, September 22-30, October 11-17, 1917; September 21-30, 1918).

Correspondents include Shmarya Levin, Louis Lipsky, Yehuda Leib Cohen, Harry Friedenwald, Horace Kallen, Arthur Ruppin, Benjamin Perlstein, Cyrus Adler, Eliyahu Lewin-Epstein, Elisha Friedman, Nahum Sokolow, Jacob De Haas, Julian Mack and James de Rothschild.

Of special interest:

copy of a letter (January 23, 1915) to Bernard Richards from Henry Morgenthau, Sr., U.S. Ambassador at Constantinople, stating that his not being an avowed Zionist enables him to act in favor of Jewish affairs in Eretz Israel, for example, arranging for a U.S. warship to bring aid to Jews in Eretz Israel; and
letter (undated, 1918) to Jacob De Haas from Weizmann, stating that strengthening the American Red Cross in Eretz Israel by sending two more units means intensification of pro-Arab activity and should therefore be avoided.

Collection also includes a letter (January 18, 1919) from David Fairchild, agricultural researcher in the U.S. Department of Agriculture to Aaron Aaronsohn, regarding the testing of new species for agriculture in Eretz Israel and educating the people in preparing the crops for the table; a letter (June 24, 1920) to Weizmann from Ephraim Ish Kishor, secretary of Judea Industrial Corporation enclosing certification of Weizmann as a shareholder; and a letter (February 28, 1915) from Samuel Pewsner informing Weizmann of a 600,000 franc loan for orange growers in Eretz Israel being collected, 1/6 of which had already been given by Jacob Schiff.

Collection also includes correspondence of Weizmann primarily with Judah L. Magnes, but also with Harry Friedenwald, Nathan Straus, Louis Lipsky, Simon Flexner, Alfred Cohen, S. J. Meltzer and Jacques Loeb concerning the following matters:

> establishment of the Hebrew University: potential contributors (File March 10-15, 1914); Nathan Straus' readiness to donate land he owns as site for the university (File February 5-14, 1914); creation of an American foundation for the university (Files February 4-28, March 6-9, 20-31, April 26-30, May, June 11-23, 1914);
>
> establishment of a scientific research institute: cooperation with Straus Health Bureau; guidance from Rockefeller Institute for Medical Research; contributions from Rockefeller Fund; opinions regarding success or failure of the proposed institute (Files February 4-14, beginning of May-6, 20-31, beginning of June-11, 11-23, July 22-26, 1914); and
>
> the Technion; announcement by Meyer Sulzberger of the decision of American members of the Technion kuratorium that Hebrew will be the language of instruction at the Technion (1914); mass meeting on behalf of the Technion; Magnes' opinion of Weizmann being a member of the kuratorium (Files March 6-9, 1914).

Three letters to Weizmann from editors of U.S. Jewish journals are also included: from Henry Hurwitz, editor of *Menorah Journal*, requesting Weizmann to write an article (File July 15, 1915); from Bernard Richards, editor of *Maccabean*, asking Weizmann's aid in obtaining a statement favorable to Zionism made by Danish critic George Brandes (File January 4, 1918); and from Cyrus Adler, editor of *Jewish Quarterly Review*, introducing the journal and suggesting that Weizmann subscribe (File December 15, 1919). Collection catalogued by repository.

Research access not restricted, but prior arrangement advisable. Photocopies provided.

TG 8/82

WORLD UNION OF ZIONISTS-REVISIONISTS

(Founded in 1925 by Zev Tiomkin; originally an integral part of the World Zionist Organization (WZO); separate branch under Zev Jabotinsky in 1933 when he called for secession from the WZO.)
Ca. 250 items, covering years 1929-1933, in Record Group G 2.
In Jabotinsky Institute in Israel, Tel Aviv.

Collection includes correspondence, mostly in English but some in Yiddish and German, between Revisionist headquarters in London and its branches in the United States (mainly New York City) dealing with the following subjects: efforts by Revisionists to increase opposition by the Zionist Organization of America (ZOA) to British policy in Palestine; determination of the Revisionists to increase their strength in the WZO, ZOA and among American Jews in general; attempts to remove both Chaim Weizmann and the opposition group led by Louis D. Brandeis; internal dissension over whether Revisionists should function within the ZOA and over the financial difficulties of the Revisionists in the United States; the split between the executive committee and Jabotinsky in 1933 and efforts by the former to rally support; and Revisionist relations with the Jewish National Fund (Folders 5/9; 6/13,15).

Of special interest are:

a letter (January 8, 1932) from Israel Baratz, secretary of Zionists-Revisionists Organization of America, expressing regret that the Jewish National Fund (JNF) has decided to deny them representation; rejecting the suggestion by JNF for representation through the Zionist Organization of America of which they do not consider themselves a part; and threatening to take steps necessary for securing their rights even if JNF collections would suffer (Folder 9/5); and

a confidential letter (March 5, 1931) from L. Altman, vice-president of the Zionists-Revisionists of America to Revisionist branches and individuals all over the country calling a protest meeting to demand the resignation of Judah L. Magnes as head of the Hebrew University, accusing Magnes of undermining the foundation of Zionism and objecting to his being considered on the same level as Vladimir Jabotinsky, "the most prominent defender of Herzlian Zionism" (Folder 9/5).

Collection catalogued by repository.
Research access not restricted. Photocopies provided.

DF 12/81

YAHUDA, ABRAHAM SHALOM, 1877-1951

(Born in Jerusalem; Orientalist; studied and taught Semitics at European universities and at the New School for Social Research in New York.)
Ca. 60 items, covering years 1933-1944, interspersed in Record Group Yah. Ms. Var. 38.
In Jewish National and University Library, Jerusalem.

Collection includes correspondence in English and German, documents, reports and newsclippings dealing with the disagreement between Europeans and Americans over the character of the Hebrew University, and the efforts of Yahuda, Albert Einstein and others to unseat Judah L. Magnes as chancellor of the university; with the Hartog Commission of Inquiry into alleged mismanagement at the university; with the financing of the university; and with criticism by Chaim Weizmann of Einstein for refusing to accept a post at the Hebrew University in 1933 (File 272).

Correspondents include Yahuda and his wife, Weizmann, Magnes, and Einstein and his wife.
Collection catalogued by repository.
Research access not restricted. Photocopies provided.

SK 3/82

YEIVIN, SHEMUEL, 1896-1982

(Archeologist; born in Russia; came to Eretz Israel 19(?); chairman of Jewish Palestine Exploration Society, 1944-1946.)
13 items, covering years 1928-1929, 1933-1940, in Record Group A 332.
In Central Zionist Archives, Jerusalem.

Collection includes personal and professional correspondence of Yeivin, mostly in Hebrew, regarding his graduate studies in Egyptology and financial aid through the Mack-Friedman Scholarship

Fund at the Hebrew University (Folder 146); and his archeological research and professional relations with American universities and publishers (Folder 144).

Correspondents include Judah L. Magnes, Leo Mayer, Cyrus H. Gordon, William F. Albright, Nelson Glueck and Solomon Grayzel.
Collection catalogued by repository.
Research access not restricted. Photocopies provided.

SG 12/81

ZEID, ALEXANDER, 1886-1938
(Born in Siberia; arrived in Eretz Israel in 1904; one of the founders of the Hashomer defense organization.)
2 items, one dated 1930 and the other undated, in Record Group 5/5.
In Yad Yitzhak Ben Zvi, Jerusalem.

Collection includes memoirs and correspondence in Hebrew and Russian mentioning the American Zion Commonwealth owning land in the Jezreel Valley and in Tabun (Tivon), and plans for leasing part to Jews and part to Arabs; and an American tailor in Mea Shearim, Jerusalem, circa 1907 (Folder 1).
Collection catalogued by repository.
Research access not restricted. Photocopies provided.

SG 2/82

SUPPLEMENT I

LEGATION IMPERIALE DE TURQUIE

Washington le 12 Mai 1898.

No. gl: 9557.
No. spl: 66

Object: Conférences israélites de New-York.

Monsieur Le Ministre,

En me référant à mon rapport du 27 Avril dernier, No 9550, 63, j'ai l'honneur d'informer Votre Excellence que l'agent secret que j'ai envoyé à New-York pour assister aux délibérations des Conférences qui devaient avoir lieu, le 10 et le 11 courant, au siége du Comité israélite de cette ville, m'a fait savoir que ces réunions avaient été remises à une date ultérieure et indéterminée, et qu'il lui a été impossible d'en connaître le motif. J'ai alors prié M. Mehemed A. R. Webb, chef de la Communauté Musulmane de New-York, de se rendre à la résidence privée du Professeur Richard Gotheil, président du comité, et de lui demander d'une manière amicale et discrète, la cause du retard apporté à la réunion des Conférences en question. Le professeur, interviewé par notre co-religionnaire américain, a déclaré, paraît-il, que c'est la guerre hispano-americaine qui a été la cause de cet ajournement et qu'aucune conférence importante ne sera peut-être plus convoquée pendant toute la duré des hostilités actuelles.

Veuillez bien agréer les assurances de la très-haute considération avec laquelle j'ai l'honneur d'être,

Monsieur Le Ministre,
de Votre Excellence,

le très-humble, dévoué serviteur

Ali Ferrouh.

SUPPLEMENT II

LEGATION IMPERIALE DE TURQUIE

Washington le 23 Juin 1898.

No. gl: 9597
No. spl: 81.

Objet: Zionisme

Monsieur Le Ministre,

    A la suite de la nomination de Monsieur Strauss, qui est un israélite allemand, au poste de Ministre Plénipotentiaire des Etats-Unis à Constantinople, les partisans de la Grande Idée Juive, dont le berceau est L'Allemagne, trouvant le moment favorable pour donner une impulsion à leur idée chimérique, ont organisé, dans ces derniers jours, plusieurs réunions où ils ont prononcé des discours et pris des résolutions concernant la Palestine. Comme ce mouvement est de nature à recevoir une forme plus politique et plus inquiétante, et à devenir "une question" pour plus tard, j'ai cru bien de prendre les mesures préventives nécessaires; et dans le but de décourager les amis de Ghetto et d'empêcher leur agissement de se propager j'ai fait publier dans les principales feuilles américaines une déclaration officieuse qui a produit une impression heureuse sur l'esprit des israélites neutres et indécis, et qui a été commentée très favorablement dans toute la presse américaine. J'ai ainsi porté un coup décisif et salutaire au "Zionisme" dont, je suis persuadé, il ne se relèvera pas facilement et presque tué le mouvement naissant. *The Jewish Messenger* de New-York, qui est l'organe le plus important du Sémitisme américain, a reproduit entièrement ma déclaration et émis une opinion dont Votre Excellence appréciera certainement la portée. J'espère qu'après avoir examiné les coupures que j'ai l'Honneur de Lui transmettre ci-incluses, Votre Excellence sera satisfaite de ma conduite à la fois sage et énergique dans cette circonstance.

Veuillez agréer les assurances de la très-haute consideration avec laquelle j'ai l'honneur d'être, Monsieur Le Ministre, de Votre Excellence, le très-humble, dévoué serviteur

Ali Ferrouh.

APPENDIX

BBA, YEE, Ç II/85-86/54/136, June 15, 1896
From Ali Ferruh, the Ottoman Delegation to Washington, to the Palace in Yildiz, Istanbul. Translated from the Turkish.

Since the ideas of the Jews about Palestine originated from German Jews and since the founding father of this movement was Theodor Herzl, a Viennese doctor, Zionists are now considering the appointment of Oscar Straus as the American Minister to Istanbul who, originally a German Jew, changed his nationality—an unexpected opportunity in facilitating the promotion of their ideas in practice. For this, they are heavily engaged in a widespread propaganda campaign, holding meetings in New York, Philadelphia and Chicago.

In order to prevent the issue assuming the color of [an international] question and to demolish their hopes and activities in the eyes of public opinion, I, without losing time, gave a declaration to the press, but I preferred to arrange it in a question and answer form which I myself wrote, not to give the impression that such an interview was deliberately sought by the Ottoman Delegation. In the paper, the original of which is despatched to the Foreign Ministry, it is stated . . .

BBA, YEE, A II 748-49/54/136, April 27, 1898.
From Ali Ferruh, the Ottoman Delegation to Washington, to the Palace in Yildiz, Istanbul. Translated from the Turkish.

The Washington Committee, a sister organization of the "Izmir Secret Association of Judaism and Zionism," as I was informed with a cable from Istanbul, is composed of 135 members under the leadership of a person called "Omil" [sic] with "Livonin" [sic] as secretary. The subscriptions collected from those American Jews who believe in the idea of the Promised Land, an annual payment of at least one dollar per person, are firstly collected by the New York Committee, the center of all committees in the States, and subsequently sent to the bank of the London committee. The New York Committee, situated at 209 Madison Avenue, is headed by Richard

Gottheil and deputied by Dr. S. Wise. When Reverend Stoden the Grand Rabbi of Washington was interviewed, he with certainty said that he belonged to the Reform School of Judaism and he had nothing to do with the ideas put forward by those who do not adhere to this same school of thought. In order to be informed about the proceedings and resolutions of the congress destined to take place on May 10-11, I would not only send an agent but have already given the necessary instructions to our consul in New York to behave in the utmost secrecy in this matter. As I have previously discussed in my report, numbered 12, His Imperial Majesty should thoroughly examine these propositions on Palestine and should take certain measures to repair the fault which his ancestors had committed by allowing the non-Muslim communities to settle in Palestine. I regret that, as I had personally observed on a recent visit to Palestine, the riches of the country are being plundered by the German and Jewish colonies. By facilitating the immigration of Muslim farmers, the Government should try to leave fewer places for the Jewish and other people. The curriculum of Jewish schools should be examined, and, apart from religious studies, all tuition should be in Turkish. The activities of Nesim Bahar, the director of the Alliance Israelite school in Jerusalem, as well as of Mr. Block and Mr. Scheid, deputies of Baron Edmond de Rothschild in Jerusalem, should be closely watched, for they, by offering amounts [of money] or other presents one could not refuse, win the support of the local Jewish population to their chimeric ideals. It must also be ensured that the land around Haram el-Sherif and the Mescid el-Aksa region in particular and the Mount Zion area in general, which they have long been craving to obtain, should never be sold to them.

BBA, YEE, Ç II/98/54/136, June 23, 1898
From Ali Ferruh, Ottoman Delegation to Washington, to the Palace in Yildiz, Istanbul. Translated from the Turkish.

In my previous letter of June 16, 1898, concerning the Zionist Association of Jewry, I had already written that my declarations were favorably received by the American public opinion which entirely agreed with me on this issue. Under these circumstances, even the papers subsidized by the Zionist Organization could not dare to come out in defense of Jewish rights. Therefore, I can assure His Imperial Majesty that, with this master stroke, I shattered the

Palestine dream of the Zionists which was becoming a serious question, and left its supporters in desperation and sorrow. The righteous-
ness and importance of my humble services in this connection would
no doubt be appreciated with the passage of time, as a New York
daily, the *Jewish Messenger*, by changing its attitude towards Zionism and by criticizing its sleep-walker coreligionists, clearly illustrates.
The above-mentioned newspaper published not only my declaration
—a copy of which is enclosed in my report to the Ministry for
Foreign Affairs—in entirety, but also a commentary whereby it
stated that the activities of those [Zionists], under the mask of
protection, might be accelerating a catastrophe, that the great body
of Israelites in America and Europe have no sympathy with Zionism
and a Jewish State, that the future of Palestine is as little a practical
question as is the millennium, that perhaps the words of the Turkish
Minister might have a salutary influence on these Don Quixotes, and
that perhaps some plainer advice might be requisite.

BBA, YEE, Ç II/275-276/54/136, January 24, 1899.
From Ali Ferruh, The Ottoman Delegation to Washington, to the
Palace in Yildiz, Istanbul. Translated from the Turkish.
  Although putting the idea of settling the Jews in Palestine in
practice could easily be discarded as a far-fetched dream, the Government of His Imperial Majesty, upon information respecting the
collection of funds and other secret activities of some evil-minded
people, studied the situation carefully and subsequently instructed
the Delegation that Jewish refugees of foreign origin would not,
under any circumstances, be allowed to enter Palestine. The Delegation, in turn, with a note dated September 9, 1898, informed and
persuaded, although with considerable difficulty, the State Department of the present Ottoman restrictions and in the same time
publicized these in the press without leaving any loopholes for
objection. Moreover, during the visit of His Majesty the Emperor
of Germany to Syria and Palestine, I had given orders, in line with
the instructions of the Sublime Porte, to all the Ottoman representatives in this country not to visae the passports of those suspicious
people who desired to visit the aforementioned countries. When the
State Department protested on behalf of those Jews to whom no
visas were issued, I used to tell the Secretary of State that, as it must
be familiar to him, all foreign Jews were forbidden entry to Palestine,

reacting to evidence that Istanbul
is weakening, under US pressure, on
exclusion of
Jewish immigrants + Pal

to which he had no choice but to acquiesce. Once the new Secretary of State appealed to me, protesting that the person to whom we declined a visa was neither a Jew, nor suspicious, but a very well known person; then I ordered the consul in New York to provide him with the papers because it was important that the American Secretary of State, by stating the applicant was not a Jew, was approving the Turkish regulations.

In a recent communication from the [Ottoman] Minister for Foreign Affairs, it has been ordered to get rid of the previous restriction, i.e., denial of visas to suspicious persons; but the restrictions placed upon Jews to enter the country have been kept in force. However, the Secretary of State, in a recent note informed me that the Minister for Foreign Affairs had agreed that the restrictions should be applied only to those Jews who came to Palestine "en masse." Therefore, he [the Secretary of State] requested me to give proper directions to the consuls to visa passports. Please have mercy on this humble soul, how he was caught in this troublesome state. All my efforts, for which I have been reaping substantial fruits, have been wasted due to the intervention of His Excellency the Minister for Foreign Affairs. Nevertheless, I told the Secretary of State that I have been waiting for some instructions from the Porte. On the other hand, I sent a telegram to the Minister for Foreign Affairs, explaining the situation, asking for instructions and requesting him to inform me in the future of his conversations with the American Minister. It has been a fortnight and he has not replied to me yet. Therefore, I protest to His Most Exalted Being, His Imperial Majesty. As the Minister for Foreign Affairs is too soft and yields to the pressures of the embassies on the one hand and to the rudeness of those brigands called dragomans on the other, he is responsible not only for the damage to His Imperial Government's prestige but also for the sacrifice of many previous accomplishments. Therefore, in order not to repeat such mistakes in the future, would it not be expedient either to have a witness during the conversations between the Minister and foreign representatives or to urge the Minister to write a report after the interview with an outline of the conversation?

In my report of October 11, 1898 (numbered 80), I had mentioned that the American Minister to Istanbul, Mr. Straus, happened to be one of the ardent supporters of the Palestine question; and that his activities should be closely scrutinized. Time has proved how right I was. I have been informed by reliable sources recently that he is continuing his persistent and sinister activities in helping the Zionists in Palestine.

I must also state that, as far as the final outcome of these policies are concerned, there would not be any difference between the entry of Jews [into Palestine] in thirties or singly, for no Hebrew visitor would declare that he is a refugee [and came to Palestine in order to settle there permanently]. Such careless [gafilâne] considerations of the Minister for Foreign Affairs would surely give birth to harmful results.

LIST OF COLLECTIONS
BY REPOSITORY

Anglo-Jewish Archives
    Myer, Henry Dennis

Archeological (Rockefeller) Museum
    Mandatory Government, Department of Antiquities, Excavations

Board of Deputies of British Jews
    Board of Deputies of British Jews

Bodleian Library
    Bryce, James, First Viscount
    Church's Ministry Among the Jews
    Fisher, Clarence S.
    Milner, Alfred, First Viscount

British and Foreign Bible Society
    American Bible Society
    British and Foreign Bible Society, Agents' Books
    British and Foreign Bible Society, Foreign Correspondence
    Malta Bible Society

Central Zionist Archives
    Auster, Daniel
    Berkson, Isaac B.
    Goldman, Solomon
    Gruenwald, Kurt
    Hertz, Joseph Herman
    Jewish Agency, Department of Education
    Kaplan, Eliezer
    Namier, Lewis Bernstein
    Radler-Feldman, Yehoshua
    Reznik (Harozen), Jacob
    Rupin, Arthur
    Sacher, Harry
    Safriel (Pisarevsky), Yeshayahu
    Sirkis, Daniel
    Tulin, Abraham
    Yeivin, Shemuel

Hakibbutz Hameuhad Archives
    Eshed, Jacob and Fruma
    Hakibbutz Hameuhad, Committee for Activities Abroad
    Hakibbutz Hameuhad, Councils
    Hakibbutz Hameuhad, Immigration and Absorption Committee
    Hakibbutz Hameuhad, Secretariat
    Merom (Mereminsky), Israel
    Singer, Mendel
    Tabenkin, Yitzhak

Israel Film Archives
    Levin, Meyer

Israel Labor Party Archives
    Mapai (Labor Party) Central Committee
    Mapai (Labor Party) Office
    Mapai (Labor Party) Secretariat, Movement Abroad
    Mapai (Labor Party) Secretariat, Protocols

Israel State Archives
    Antonius, George
    Emergency Committee (Jewish Agency and Vaad Leumi)
    Germany, Consulates in Palestine
    Great Britain, Consulate in Jerusalem
    Leassirenu (Prisoners' Welfare Society)
    Levy, Joseph
    Mandatory Government, Administrator General
    Mandatory Government, Attorney General
    Mandatory Government, Chief Secretary's Office
    Mandatory Government, Department of Agriculture and Fisheries
    Mandatory Government, Department of Education
    Mandatory Government, Department of Health
    Mandatory Government, Department of Migration
    Mandatory Government, Director of Customs and Excise
    Mandatory Government, District Commissioner's Office, Jerusalem
    Mandatory Government, District Commissioner's Office, Lydda
    Mandatory Government, Public Works Department
    Mandatory Government, Railways and Ports Administration
    Mandatory Government, Registrar of Cooperative Societies
    Samuel, Edwin Herbert, Second Viscount
    Samuel, Herbert Louis, First Viscount

Jabotinsky Institute in Israel
    African Exiles' Archive
    Akzin, Benjamin
    American Friends of a Jewish Palestine
    Anglo-American Committee for a Jewish Army, London
    Anglo-American Committee for a Jewish Army, New York
    Arlosoroff Murder Trial, Non-Partisan Committee for the Defence
    Ben Horin, Eliyahu
    Emergency Committee to Save the Jewish People of Europe
    Gilner, Elias
    Grossman, Meir
    Hebrew Committee of National Liberation
    Hecht, Ben
    Irgun Zevai Leumi, Diaspora Staff, Paris
    Jabotinsky, Eri
    Jabotinsky, Zev (Vladimir)
    Jewish Legionnaires' Association of America
    Jewish State Party, World Executive Committee, Tel Aviv
    Kook, Hillel (Peter Bergson)
    Kopelowicz, Aharon
    Leassirenu (Prisoners' Welfare Society)
    Lohamei Herut Israel (LEHI or Stern Group)
    New Zionist Organization, Presidency, London
    New Zionist Organization, Presidency, United States Delegation
    NILI
    Patterson, John Henry
    Plugoth Haavoda (Work Brigades) of Betar
    Rosoff, Israel
    Seligman, Max (Law Office)
    United Zionists-Revisionists, World Secretariat, Paris
    World Union of Zionists-Revisionists

Jewish National and University Library
    Epstein, Zalman
    Hacohen, Mordechai Ben Hillel
    Haffkine, Waldemar Mordecai
    Hamizrachi-Hovevei Zion in Russia
    Hebrew University, Congratulatory Scrolls
    Irgun Zevai Leumi, Diaspora Staff, Paris
    Jerusalem Kollelot
    Masliansky, Zvi Hirsch
    Schwadron Collection of Autographs and Portraits, Einstein Files
    Yahuda, Abraham Shalom

Lambeth Palace Library
    Blyth, George Francis Popham
    Jerusalem and East Mission/Fund

Ottoman State Archives
    Turkey, Archives of the Foreign Office
    Turkey, Archives of the Prime Minister's Office (Basbakanalik Arsivi)

Palestine Exploration Fund
    Palestine Exploration Fund, Excavations
    Palestine Exploration Fund, Western Survey of Palestine

Public Record Office
    Great Britain, Cabinet Memoranda and Papers
    Great Britain, Colonial Office, Palestine Correspondence
    Great Britain, Foreign Office, Embassy and Consular Archives
    Great Britain, Foreign Office, Embassy Archives and High Commission, Egypt
    Great Britain, Foreign Office, Embassy Archives, Turkey
    Great Britain, Foreign Office, General Correspondence, Turkish Empire to 1905
    Great Britain, Foreign Office, General Correspondence, United States to 1906
    Great Britain, Foreign Office, General Political Correspondence
    Great Britain, Foreign Office, News Department
    Great Britain, State Papers Foreign, Archives of British Legations
    Great Britain, War Cabinet and Cabinet, Minutes
    Great Britain, War Cabinet and Cabinet, Registered Files

Rhodes House Library
    Chancellor, Sir John Robert

St. Anthony's College Middle East Centre
    American Colony in Jerusalem
    Dickson, John
    Jerusalem and East Mission/Fund
    Keith-Roach, Edward

Tel Aviv-Yaffo Municipality Historical Archives
    Aaronsohn Family

Theater Archives
    Habimah Theater

University of Birmingham Library
    Church Missionary Society

Weizmann Archives
    Weizmann, Chaim

Yad Yitzhak Ben Zvi
    American Colony in Jerusalem
    Ben Avi, Ithamar
    Ben Ze'ev (Abramovitch) Family
    Ben Zvi, Yitzhak
    Binyamini, Yosef
    History of the Yishuv
    Joseph, Dov (Bernard)
    Lampert and Gelman Families
    Levanon (Bellinsky) Family
    Nadav (Halpern), Zvi
    Sukenik, Eliezer Lipa
    Zeid, Alexander

INDEX TO VOLUME 4

tee, 110, 136
American Jewish Relief Committee, 147
American League for a Free Palestine, 7, 72, 75, 77, 130
American Palestine Engineers, 142
American Palestine Exploration Society, 125
American Palestine Institute, 86
American Palestine Real Estate Agency, 17
American Schools of Oriental Research, 110
American Zionist Bureau, 42
American Zion Commonwealth, 15, 17, 19, 73, 105, 139, 141, 152
American Zionist Emergency Council, 2, 22, 70, 74, 84, 146
American Zionist Medical Unit, 56, 60
Americans for Haganah, 91
Anglo-American Committee of Inquiry, 12, 20, 28, 70, 74, 80, 87, 90, 94, 95, 109, 113, 131, 133
Anglo-American Jewish Association, 110
Anglo-American Society, 110
Anglo-Egyptian Bank, 58
Anglo-Palestine Company, 23
Antonius, George, 8-13, 64
Arab-Jewish Relations, 9, 21, 32, 74, 92-93, 97, 108, 129, 133, *see also* Brit Shalom
Arab riots, 22, 32, 58, 64, 68, 90, 113, 114
Archaeology, 33, 36, 40, 46, 98-102, 124-125, 138, 152
Arlosoroff, Chaim, 14, 78, 113
Armstrong, George, 125-126
Assirei Zion Committee, 136
Assirei Zion Fund, 70, 136
Attlee, Clement, 89
Auster, Daniel, 14
Austin, Warren R., 76

Bade, William, 98, 100
Baeck, Leo, 129
Bailey, H. W., 35
Baldwin, Mary B., 34
Balfour, Arthur, 12, 23, 44-45, 54, 56, 59, 60, 61, 135
Balfour Declaration, 11, 12, 31, 42, 57, 61, 62, 78, 83, 134, 147
Balfouriya, 5, 23
Baratz, Israel, 63, 150
Baratz, Joseph, 113
Barclay, Colville, 54, 56
Barclay, James, 49, 50-51, 53
Bardin, Shlomo, 102-103
Barker, Benjamin, 30, 60
Barker, John, 60
Batty, T., 81
Bean, Jacob D., 6
Beauboucher, Victor, 40
Beaumont, E. F., 101
Beer Toviya, 26
Ben-Aharon, Yitzhak, 66, 68, 139
Ben-Ami, Oved, 15
Ben-Ami, Yitzhak, 7, 77
Ben-Avi, Ithamar, 14-17
Ben Eliezer, Arieh, 7, 38
Ben Gurion, David, 19-20, 41, 74, 85, 87, 105, 109, 111, 113, 114, 115, 116, 118, 137
Ben-Horin, Eliyahu, 17-18, 121
Ben-Tov, Mordechai, 133
Ben Yehuda, Eliezer, 17, 65
Ben Yehuda, Hemda, 17
Ben-Zvi, Rachel Yanait, 20
Ben-Zvi, Yitzhak, 18-21, 26, 105
Bennett, Courtney, 54, 56
Bension, Max, 58
Benson, Edward, 81
Bentwich, Norman, 9, 54, 96, 103, 120, 129
Bergson, Peter, 5, 6, 7, 37, 38, 70-71, 76, 89, 123
Berkson, Isaac B., 21-25, 73

INDEX TO VOLUMES 1–3

Goldenberg, Salomon, II, 63
Goldman, Frank, II, 87
Goldman, Julius, II, 159
Goldman, Max, I, 12
Goldman, Reuben, II, 19
Goldman, Simon, I, 24, 26, 49, 71, 81
Goldman, Solomon, I, 52; II, 18, 21,
    31, 90, 140, 176, 196; III, 128
Goldmann, Nahum, II, 19, 20, 50, 52,
    71, 92, 98, 121, 176, 199; III,
    8, 125
Goldsmith, Gertrude, III, 91
Goldsmith, Lester, III, 49
Goldstein, Benjamin F., II, 35
Goldstein, Israel, II, 52, 65, 152, 184,
    186, 189
Goldwater, A., III, 107
Goodell, William, I, 5
Gordon, Aharon David, II, 64
Gordon, Samuel, I, 94
Gordonia Youth Organization, II, 64
Gottheil, Emma, I, 95; II, 81, 150
Gottheil, Gustav, II, 81
Gottheil, Richard, I, 110; II, 33, 36,
    37, 42, 47, 50, 55, 61, 64-65,
    80-81, 132, 176; III, 128
Gourich, Paul, II, 36
Gout, Jean, II, 17
Graisel, John Stanley, II, 184
Grand, Samuel, II, 65
Grand Mufti, I, 84
Granott (Granovsky), Abraham, I, 36;
    II, 65-66
Gratz family, III, 72
Great Britain, II, 66-76
Green, William, II, 46, 136, 143
Greenberg, Chaim, II, 24, 73, 76
Grew, Joseph C., II, 76-77, 144
Gross, Joel, II, 18
Grossman, Harry, II, 65
Grossman, Meir, III, 16-17
Gruenbaum, Itzhak, II, 54, 92
Gruenwald, Kurt, III, 17, 37

Gugenheimer Playgrounds, I, 26
Gunther, John, II, 143
Gutheim, James K., III, 94
Guthrie, John Julius, I, 37

Habonim, I, 37-38
Hadani-Rafaeli, Alexander, II, 133
Hadassah, I, 38-39, 67, 95; II, 19, 23,
    24, 32, 37, 49, 77-79, 91, 93,
    96, 114-115, 118, 119, 120, 121,
    131, 136, 145, 149-151, 152,
    187, 194, 195, 196, 198; III, 57,
    66, 68, 70, 71, 73-94, 102, 103,
    105, 122, 123, 127, 130
Hadassah Medical Organization, I, 23,
    26, 38, 42, 54, 92, 95, 115, 118
Haganah, II, 19, 50, 171; III, 67
Haggai, Jeremiah, I, 29, 39
Ha-Ikar Hatzair, I, 26, 72, 80
Hakibbutz Hameuhad, III, 18
Halberstam, Yehezkel Shraga, I, 86
Halifax, Lord, II, 20, 66, 68, 69, 70,
    74
Halperin, Rose, II, 37; III, 74, 81
Halpern, Michael, III, 49
Hamashbir Hamerkazi, III, 36
Hamilton, Marian, I, 71
Hamlin, Isaac, II, 31; III, 40
Hankin, Yehoshua, I, 39
Hannush, Victoria, I, 106
Hanoteah, III, 8
Hantke, Dr., II, 91, 183
Harding, Warren G., II, 90, 100, 191
Harlap, Yaakov, III, 111
Harman, Zena, III, 76
Harmon, Arthur L., I, 112
Harris, Zelig, II, 47
Harrisburg, Pa., II, 1
Harrison, Austin St. B., III, 109
Harrison, Leland, II, 179
Harry Fischel Institute, III, 33
Hart, Abraham, III, 63
Harte, Archibald C., I, 14, 74, 112, 113